kill
or
cure

On the Wing

O My Life!

Giant Night

Baby Breakdown

No Hassles

West Indies Poems

Life Notes

Self-Portrait (with Joe Brainard)

Fast Speaking Woman

Memorial Day (with Ted Berrigan)

Journals & Dreams

Sun the Blonde Out

Shaman

Polar Ode (with Eileen Myles)

Countries

Cabin

First Baby Poems

Sphinxeries (with Denyse Du Roi)

Makeup on Empty Space

Invention (with drawings by Susan Hall)

Skin Meat Poems

The Romance Thing

Den Monde in Farbe Sehen

Blue Mosque

Shaman/Shamane

Tell Me About It: Poems for Painters

Helping the Dreamer: New & Selected Poems

Her Story (with lithographs by Elizabeth Murray)

Not a Male Pseudonym

Lokapala

Fait Accompli

Troubairitz

Iovis

Suffer the Mysterium

Kill or Cure

kill
or
cure

Anne Waldman

PENGUIN POETS

PENGUIN BOOKS
Published by the Penguin Group
Penguin Books USA Inc., 375 Hudson Street,
New York, New York 10014, U.S.A.
Penguin Books Ltd, 27 Wrights Lane, London W8 5TZ, England
Penguin Books Australia Ltd, Ringwood, Victoria, Australia
Penguin Books Canada Ltd, 10 Alcorn Avenue,
Toronto, Ontario, Canada M4V 3B2
Penguin Books (N.Z.) Ltd, 182–190 Wairau Road,
Auckland 10, New Zealand

Penguin Books Ltd, Registered Offices:
Harmondsworth, Middlesex, England

First published in Penguin Books 1994

1   3   5   7   9   10   8   6   4   2

Some of the writing in this book first appeared in the following magazines and
anthologies: *The American Poetry Review, Big House, Conjunctions, Homage to Frank
O'Hara, The Little Magazine, The New Censorship, Nocturnal Missions, Notus,* "O"
Anthology, The Portable Beat Reader, edited by Ann Charters (Penguin Books),
*Resurgent, Rolling Stock, The Shambhala Sun, Stiletto, Talisman, Taos Review, That
Various Field* (for James Schuyler), *The 13th Moon,* and *The World.* The author
expresses special gratitude to the following presses that have published some of the
work: The Alternative Press, Apartment Editions (Hanover, Germany), Bamburger
Books, Boog Press, Kulchur Foundation, Last Generation Press, Munich Editions,
Rocky Ledge Cottage Editions, Stonehill Publishing Co., Tender Buttons, United
Artists, and Z Press.

Author's Note
With appreciation to the following individuals for their support in publishing the work:
Bill Bamburger, Lee Ann Brown, Reed Bye, Mark DuCharme, Kenward Elmslie, Lita
Hornick, Alice Notley, Ute and Jurgen Schmidt, Ivan Suvanjieff, and Lewis Warch.
Thanks to Michael Coe for useful Maya information. Additional bows to Maureen and
Robert Hunter and to my editor, David Stanford.

Author photograph by Gary Mackender

Library of Congress Cataloging in Publication Data
Waldman, Anne, 1945–
Kill or cure / Anne Waldman.
p.   cm.—(Penguin poets)
ISBN 0 14 058.708 X
I. Title.
PS3573.A4215K5   1994
811'.54—dc20   93-48917

Printed in the United States of America
Set in Electra
Designed by Claire Naylon Vaccaro

for andrew schelling
guardian & scribe

"Thee?" Oh, "Thee" is who cometh first
Out of my own soul-kin,
For I am homesick after mine own kind
And ordinary people touch me not.

—EZRA POUND

A Note

That bird—that sounded nearly human—what was it? Or who? And bend your ear, poet, to the rain forest jungle ground as well, all the rustlings, gestures, motions of life, contrasted to rough-weathered stone-hewn pyramid, elegant you could say, and noisy. Surely you hear the architecture of it, climbing to the stars? The aspiration of it? For it was important to understand the calendrical cycles, the comings and goings of Venus, yet noticing Venus was the same object, evening and morning, morning and evening. Noticing his or her (for Venus seems not male nor female in this version of influence) slaughters, discontents, eclipses, ellipses, changed & fixed mood in the ebb & flux of internal weaves, machinations, conquistador conquest, surprise. A rude awakening for those who inhabited the dream.

Could I ever "let" my blood as they purportedly did? I wonder. Literally, no. Drawn from the tongue? But you pour that blood symbolically onto the virgin page, scribed with brush or turkey feathers dipped in black or red paint contained in conch-shell inkpots. And then bind those pages with a jaguar-skin cover. La Ruta Maya.

This codex is never lazy. It wishes to be a mere script of and for a dreamer who dwelt in a prosperous/desperate turn of century, torqued by doubt, fear, imagination, passion. Let it be said she was a raging insomniac.

"Kill or cure" is a psychological nexus of negative capability, an old Tantric notion. To hold simultaneous thoughts, often seemingly contradictory thoughts, in the mind, without "any irritable reaching after fact and reason." It is the battle cry, the underpinning of a tragic age as well as going way back to primordial cellular reaches of *how things move*. It is, in the whispered oral lineage, kill *and* cure, which seems cruel for relative quotidian action and implies power little understood by this writer. Kill ego's greedy grasping, its whine and agression. Ego's self-perpetuation is the sacrificial victim, the corpse you stomp upon. As it dies, you are simultaneously cured and live on, transformed, rewired. An old shamanic trick. Isn't that enough task for one planet's aggressive nature? You kill or cut out like the surgeon what's unnecessary, all those toxins, cancers, dark attitudes, shed the endometrium, then heal the rest. To survive. You get the picture. But because we live in a dark age beset with dualities and because time is precious, one makes a choice. Kill or cure. Against or for. It is ethos that beckons. Stuff of poetry? Ha! You might laugh. Words may either kill or cure as well, who hasn't felt their deadly sting or balm? As a further note and pun, the Tibetan word for mandala is *kyil khor*. Kyil means center, and khor means fringe or surrounding area: gestalt. It's a way of looking at situations in terms of relative truth. *If that exists, this exists; if this exists, that exists.* Center and fringe are interdependent situations. Killing or curing are interdependent situations. You can't have one without the other.

As grizzled cracked-voiced Andy Devine would say in quaint grainy celluloid Western over a tin cup of cowboy coffee laced with home-made hootch, "It'll either kill or cure ya!"

> Jade eyes of the jaguar
>   the last thing you saw
> or
> wall of skulls
> & which of these
> out of all of these
>   something (one?) startled awake
> Chac needs blood this century too
>
>   Venus conjunct
> cat-like tongues & penises
> spurt ("let") onto bark
>
> it is written
> it is written

This book is a composite of journals, travel pieces, vignettes, political rants, credos, manifestos, love songs, dreams, meditations, visitations from male-writer-ghost ancestors, homages to the great women poets, and other states of mind and occasion. As such it is a body of both quotidian and imaginary realities. It is a *cento* of my mind and mind's musical making. It's also what's *on my mind*. . . . A sampler. A patchwork of day and night. The book is organized through the basic instincts of tone and impulse and runs not always parallel to linear time. Rather moves randomly yet to great purpose from the Yucatán to Bali to Quebec City to Tehran to Managua to Germany to Toulouse to New York City to Oslo to Hawaii to Miami and Dallas and many spots in between, ending somewhere near May 1993 scattering my father's ashes over a lake in southern New Jersey, USA, followed by another Maya meditation. The book spans a world of attention.

A.W.

August 11, 1993 / Cobá, Quintana Roo

Contents

kill
or
cure

Suppose a Game

Suppose language is a game
    whose rules are dreamed
        by an agreement of players

Once broken, the speakers are tossed
    & know no rude tongue but their own
        no (fixed) meaning in solipsism

But always in a process of being stranded
    are spectators of solipsism
        stuck with themselves, empirical data

Theirs is private demon language
    obstruction, ownership, demand
        Is the door open?

Rain here yet?
    Have their ideas entered all heads?
        Is this the end of the game?

They quickly become the ex-modern
    and you, poet, enter the arena
        an animating principle to a touch of words

Seduce them to your page
    caress plosiveness
        beat them a fine shapelessness

Or sentences are for the first time stark & clear
    not untrue to what flaunts style:
        webs of cloth, a mirror you hold

The players conjure nihilism, their only way
        to be curious, vain, a waste of strength
                as confusion weakens the vocal art

Cybernetics is the exchange of their news for yours
        Yours is: However abundant the nectar,
                the bees stop dancing as the sugar drops

They tell you nothing, their lips are sealed, you keep dancing
        Was the agreement that words shine like sun,
                or glint as weapons in moonlight?

A Name as Revery

Ate the bare limbs of words
to find my name:

of fevers, of trees it's made

Choice out of jugular to be born
Centuries of solar flowers gone by
Belle, where ya born? Moi? Moi?

Verdict: tens attend to
doubt all doubt as
La Self errs in revenge

Then ravages in a kind of honor umbrage

Although American
to a haute parentage we swing
John of the Hands & Waldemann's was my father
LeFevre, my mother, exposed in sandals & silk

Her Night

Out of an eye comes research
Her night: portrait & a description
A night of knowledge was plainly hers
Two ways of writing explain this
There was her night
And then there was her night, a repetition
A night in a quarry in Helena, Montana, was not anticipated
Or at dusk before the night had started:
　　The Lavender Open Pit Copper Mine near Bisbee
Everywhere she claims it as hers: purple, dark, starry
Buffalo: spring snow
Amherst: Emily Dickinson's night, what was that?
Night is anyone's guess
Naming the stars & planets: Saturn still extant after all this time
So I went on with an idea of the night
Djuna's night
All-American nights
Recesses one has one's program for
She dreamed her clothes were like Spanish ice cream
She dreamed a moth arrived to convey a scarlet secret
It was a female moth
The mosquitoes protested they were female too
She had the desire to include a shawl & Kleenex
She walked where there had never been a mountain
　　Can you be sure?
　　Can you be that sure?
She would think about walking to Sanitas Mountain at night
If any thought about night or place with night inside it is left out
　　she's sorry
For she can't even begin to remember the rooms:
　　El Rito, Bellevue, La Quinta, the old man's stuffy sitting room
She was lost in the abstraction of the girl's perfume
Nights in front of a shrine prostrating to her potentially
　　luminous mind

Sleeping late
Literature is being written at night
The couchette rattles into Trieste
A plane jets across the continent
Now I am above the clouds & the moon is up with me
Seeing what someone else means by night is another option
There was her night, and then there was her night, a repetition
She picked up the telephone while, she, the other,
    walked toward a mountain
There was her night and then there was her night—the other's—a
    repetition
She suspends all preconceptions and forgets the concept "moon"
It could be frightening if you were a prisoner
Or, a relief
Her night is of no importance really
But there has never been another one like it
Moonlight: hear the amorous cats
Moonlight: the South American map lies on the hammock
    exposed to the elements
She did not "drop by" at 1 a.m. as supposed
But made another night call
A bird called
Confused by jet lag, time went out of her control
She shrugged & went to a party
Her escort parked the car near Coit Tower
In between lovers
Between textures: silk, velvet, cool cotton
Throw back the bedspread!
Out of the eye comes the moon
Out of the eye: seduction
What does it really matter what anyone does
There was her night
And then there was her night, a repetition
Minnesota is just like that
She wouldn't give out her address in Oregon
Her coat was made for a night like this
Her night: where was it leading?

None knew
Display her zeal hour by hour
Opium would change this dream
Her nervousness was a blind
Talk about something like: "We in this period have not
    lived in remembering" or
"My excitement is my open eyes"
Her clothing is of a daily-island-life variety
A line distinguishes it
She almost traveled to Tent City out of love & honor
Everything will have to be repeated in the morning
Listen: hum of typewriter, Jacqueline's loud refrigerator & clock
Listen: a long line of thoughts bargaining to enter in
One thought: the time is 3:15 a.m.
Another thought: there is only one way to phone her
And another: night is long to her & short to us
Not at all
She is ahead of herself but behind every action
Concentration was like having the night inside her all the time she said
She said she'd go to any length to stay awake, imbibing controlled
    substances as well as caffeine
She said this because she was excited about making double time
It was her night and then it was her night a repetition
This is an ordinary great deal to know

Of Ah Or

I cannot be but
fierce
My tongue—is it so?
& liaison of that tight
pact of
this to that
A bargain
rises
swells
reigns
sends darts North
when it is you,
iced over,
I thrust
in my heart
to consider
All the vowels
sing how to
melt that glare
or
stare into
doubt like
words in a
bubble
Can't back out
now
but sing to you
a fire across
our divide,
my tongue is forked!
Flesh language!
We fall into
pieces of
the painting

to be
put
in motion
Splash or Freeze
of Ah or
Whelp
Tell to
        old Greeks
who knew
to stress
(pounce)
stretch out
as you your limbs
the statues tell us
Move it! Move it!
& the Ode
got danced
Tell it to poet
whatshername
Heliodora?
who sang
& shook her ankles,
swallowed honey
to make
a sweeter sound or
Ah, Macabru
I tune your lyre
Stomp on the page!

Speech you are golden
Speech you crack ope my skull
Speech you lieth not down a while
but even as I dream
you rouse me
Rock bed!
Break into babe increments
prick ear awake

8

Spit juice in my face
Fricative magic excites
every corpuscle
Implode & regroup
Assail me with
all yr plans
to consider
the length & shadow
of vowels

American wags listen
The East is yearning for resurrection
The West is underdeveloped
I want to ride you out here
under Big Sky
Rail 'gainst acid rain,
cruelty, weird belief systems
Insult those who do you
no good in their squawk & bite

Who serve you poorly in
their bid for glory
condemned
'fore they
even sputter forth

What goddess will abide a dull,
          ignorant tongue?

I speak it

You play me
that forms it

Quote Captive

New sleep uptorn,
Wakeful suspension between dream and dream—
                                            —LAURA RIDING

Orbits of intertextual modern talk
    now poetic, now skeptical,
now written down for human hands to hold,
    or sensibly dropped, or squirm and die
now rise again. What do you do?
    And to deserve them? Night goes down . . .
What do you choose? An object for my verb . . .
    Who let you in? The mysterious animal . . .
Who are you rooting for? A dream . . .
    Born to talk? And sing and write this down . . .

Wait for the place to be abounding in decision
    or shaft all strategies. Scratch them?
Conversation isn't cheap here, it's looming,
    precious, sacred, clumsy, inept
Wait for them—the words or concepts is it?—to be
    newly minted then strike. Terrorize the terminology
Lunar, linear, arch, lingering under cover of bed
    They could be my sisters, those buddy thoughts
They could be addressing the new populism
    or undressing old idioms

Cluster round. This is the clutter
    of mind I offer an argument to
Singular masters take heed the goad's unstoppable
    or make your way clear to surrender her light
A woman rises in Houston, sets in Michigan
    and never sleeps. Oh tempt a strapping mind . . .

A thought is mangled in the wrong hands
    because it oversteps a sleep-boundary
Necessary to speak although you might
    never know the mastery of sleep

Now sing and write this down

Jack Kerouac Dream

He's talking speedily about the evil of the feminine but he likes it. O
bitter tones of the demon feminine. He's in a repressed New England
winter room, but oddly it's like the old whorehouse in Eldora with bats
inside the walls. There's peeling wallpaper of gold fleur-de-lys pattern
on green on the far side. And his "coat of arms," or rather "his mother's
arm coat (arm chair?)" is close by. It looks like a shrunken deer's head,
size of a rabbit's foot with French letters crudely scrawled on a wooden
plaque beneath, "est peur" (translates "is fear" but cognate to, or
sounds like, "espoir"—hope). He's shivering in an old camel's hair coat,
smoking—Chesterfields? Old Golds?—in front of a raging fire. He's
wanting to "hunt and gather," he says, but it's too cold. Where can we
go to forage now that "all the skies are broken"? I am thinking if only
I were born earlier I could love him, take care of him. Close to his face
now, I see its raging corpuscles in the dancing firelight. Intricate ab-
origine designs tattooed on a remarkably pristine visage. "It's a drift,
flesh and bone, mortification, deadpan, life's a raked field," he mum-
bles. I'm part of a Buddhist plot to get him to be reborn to "liberate
all sentient beings." I'm inviting him to give a reading at The Academy
of the Meticulous Future. But what may I offer? "I tried calling your
phone was dead was why I came." "Ummm." He's off somewhere else,
his eyes moist and glassy.

April Dream

I'm with Frank O'Hara, Kenward Elmslie & Kenneth Koch visiting
Donald Hall's studio or lab (like Ivy League fraternity digs) in "Old Ann
Arbor." Lots of drink & chitchat about latest long poems & how do
we all rate with Shakespeare. Don is taking himself very seriously &
nervously as grand host conducting us about the place. It's sort of class
reunion atmosphere, campus history (Harvard?) & poetry business to
be discussed. German mugs, wooden knickknacks, prints, postcards dec-
orate the room, Kenward making snappy cracks to me about every little
detail. Where's John Ashbery? We notice huge panels of Frank O'Hara
poems on several walls and Kenneth reads aloud: "a child means
BONG" from "Biotherm." We notice more panels with O'Hara works,
white on red—very prettily shellacked, à la Chinoise—& translated by
Ted Berrigan. Slogan-like lines: "THERE'S NOBODY AT THE CONTROLS!"
"NO MORE DYING." Frank is very modest about these displays and not
altogether present (ghost). Then Don unveils a huge series of additional
panels, also painted on wood, that he's collecting for a huge catalogue-
anthology for which Frank O'Hara is writing the introduction. They
seem to be copies of Old Masters, plus Cubist, Abstract Expressionist
works, plus Jasper Johns, Joe Brainard collages & George Schneeman
nudes. Frank has already compiled a list or "key," but we're all sup-
posed to guess what each one is or at least the source of each, like a
parlor game. The panels and list are both like a scroll covered with soft
copper which peels back.

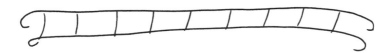

I wonder what I am doing with this crowd of older men playing a
guessing game. None of us are properly naming the "sources," Kenneth
the most agitated about this.

Then the "key" is revealed and the first 2 on it are:

I. Du Boucheron

II. Jean du Jeanne Jeanne le Boucheron  (wineglass)

"I knew it! I knew it!" shouts Kenneth.

We are abruptly distracted from the game by children chorusing "da da da du DA LA" over & over again, very guileless & sweet. We all go to a large bay window which looks over a grade-school courtyard. Frank says, "Our youth."

June Dream

I am a three-dimensional map for Doctor "Sneakers" Burroughs. The Doctor is examining the map closely with a large eye glass. It's projected above, over his head. I am pointing out the veins on the map, saying, "Look there, look there . . ." (King Lear's dying speech) very slowly and majestically. The word "spreadeagled" appears in my head to define the map. The veins are oddly feathery, delicate, & a luminescent blue-green peacock color. Presently I notice from my position above there are others forming a mandala around the Doctor.

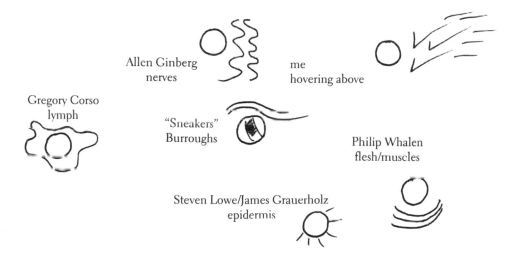

"Sneakers" is checking them out as they offer themselves as 3-D maps. Allen Ginsberg is "just a bundle of nerves"—like a big ball of heavy-duty-wire cable. Gregory Corso represents lymph. There's always the subtle detail that makes these recognizable to real life: Allen's gaping eyes from paralyzed side of face (he's had bout with Bell's palsy), Gregory's Rembrandtian hair & ruddy cheek, Philip Whalen's buddha-belly. Steven Lowe & James Grauerholz are more opaque and illusive. They are the smallest bundle, meshed together, and are summed up in the phrase "billysboys" (they are Burroughs' secretaries in real life). I recognize my own left vein under the Doctor's magnifying glass. He's making sucking sounds as he walks, slightly bent, around the mandala studying each bundle laboriously, a big blue animal-like (insect) eye enlarged behind the glass. The glass turns into a full-blown miner's mask. These bundles of people are now like boulders which make me think of "bones" and I wonder Where is, who is Bones? Burroughs himself? Words: disemboned, disemboweled, disembodied. I am attracted toward the skin bundles to protect my veins. Doc "Sneakers" is saying "Well, yes, well, hmmmmm, sure, take a broaaaaaad general view" in a withering tone, as he circles the mandala. The boulder-people-bundles are now pulsating in their respective spots, like kinetic sculptures. Allen is writhing in a most terrifying manner (turns black & blue with red sparks flying), Gregory is a sculpture of green neon, I'm a tangle of blue wires, Philip is quivering jelly, while Steven & James are fluttering like silk. My heart chakra is imploding with all this activity. There's the pressure of blood coursing through my veins and I feel a tremendous gushing toward the whole situation, physically & emotionally. Now the "spirits" of the boulders like me are hovering above. I can feel their presences, but no longer see them. The phrase "Love's fire heats water, water cools not love" also from Shakespeare and spoken in same King Lear dying voice as before startles the Doctor who now sucks himself away like a black hole and disappears at the exact center of the mandala—down a trapdoor! This whole scene has been taking place on a stage set for "The Magic Mountain Movie." I think to myself: What shall I do down there, at the Remember Some Apartments? I awake with the task to go boil water, for coffee, for tea.

Old Dream Ritual

We did this in several dreams in our twenties I remember to find the
  origin of "book." Remember?

Sister Bernadette is heckling me
No, my sister, support me
And my sister raises me up
She plays the piano,
Her music accompanies my life
We're on stage
Bright spotlights on us
Sister wearing the dress I gave you
On the stage of our lives
"Etonne-moi, sister," I cry
I have the book! I have my book!
My book, this one,
the one in the black binder, you remember
Remember, sister?
The book of our life
Infuriating black binder, never binding enough
Pages, texts, works, poetry, her heartbroken
family lineage stories
Old drama, the story of you
The story of you & me, remember?
We fell in love to change the world, remember?
A book book book book to change the world, remember?
Middle English *beche* from Old English *bēce*, akin to O Frisian *bōk*,
OE and Old Saxon *bōc*, *bōk*, Old High German *buohha* (G *Buche*)
Old Norse *bōk*, beech
Old Slavic *bŭzŭ*, elm
L. *fāgus*, beech
Gr. *phēgos*, edible oak
The OE variant *bōc*, *bōk* became ME *bok*, *book*,
English *book*
Gothic *bōka*, letter of alphabet

pl. *bōkōs*
documents, books
Originally beech-wood sticks on which runes were carved
(repeat these origins after me: *beche, bēce, bōc, bōk, bouhha,* etc.)
On stage:
A theater carved like the Entermedia
Made of women bones
Enter the media
We are ready for them,
We can make up the stories of our lives
They will believe anything about wild-speaking women
We were there once
All the women performers carving a circle around William Burroughs:
Laurie, Patti, Bernadette, Anne
and then one (you are that one) become my sister
and then it's my turn
Break out of the circle, go to my book
It's as big as the world

"I am blinded by a fiery circle"

for James Schuyler

It is summer 1970
You've "gone mad"
You're washing
dollar bills
in the bathtub
& hanging them out
on the clothesline
in Southhampton to dry
You write to me
"money is shit"
Your handwriting
is angry, stubborn
Then you send
another note:
"I'll support you" &
"don't worry"
This is puzzling

Then
one point
at the board game
(with Kenward & Joe
in Vermont)
head split in
my hands sore
with your suffering
O Jimmy

Which breakdown
later
Payne Whitney:
venetian blinds

willfully shut
Your fingernails are
long, bent as a witch's
Tufts of
blunt brow hair
leap
above your eyes
which roll back
cunningly
Breath comes in
clumps, "medicated"

Tongue-parched
demon inside you
great poet,
rages
What's his fear?

"How *is* it outside?"
you ask
This will help
I go to open
the blinds thinking,
this *helps*
"No, don't do it"
(desperate)

"Too bright!"

A Guston

homage to Philip Guston,
1913–1980

a skeletal guardian, a hungry ghost, a mafia man, an old implant,
weathered shoes, the stockmarket crash of 1929, mural eye,
narrative you could say like his dream, Moses' tablets,
commandmcnts of a lightbulb, deity of thc street, the kitchen,
pay dirt, hit the pavement, gone, ricochet of time,
nostalgia for the-morning-after, what ring of Dante's hell?

ring of sweat, odd laboratory, desire and villainy, sainthood
not about niceties, proper shoes, wanted to lie down with the
setting sun, wanted to be one with the place, Samuel Beckett
stopped here, this was a childhood, this was a nightmare,
this was what the World War could do, a man stood up,
a man stood down, a man stood up, a man stood down, a man

holier than a tree, holier than a mistake, holier than food,
barrenness, wantonness, the glee of the comic book, it was
a movie, a motion picture show, a matinee, it was the bites
in his life, it was rhapsody, it was solo jazz, reminder to sleep,
it was the insomniac's revenge, it was his own mind talking,
the sun came up, the earth stood still, the paint at the tip of

brushes? implants? eyeballs? a wink, a stare, a bald lie,
dramaturgy, the paint was talking to you, hungry ghosts
in the bardo, an eggshell light, a warm tangent, a litany
of disasters, were they, the mob, responsible? who snitched?
celluloid is speeding up life, someone still smoked a cigar,
in the center of his life all the details showed one heart-risk.

Love of His Art

for Joe Brainard

I have not mastered cinematic intelligence
Screen gone,
Each little mannerism aspen shuddering:
    the storm is here! the storm is here!

Keep even smoothness spread out
like the eye keeps track of sun going in
& out of clouds. Then 2 clouds crash.

The world is going at a nomad's pace
its face you find routine
& then, surprise
none other than I experience
finding you. This is what does happen
beauty ringing the ear,
      vernacular

I hope you see how crucial intrusions are
for what I mean may be clearer more insistent
because my eyes sigh in debt to yours.

When the World Was Steady

No matter how hard I try
to forget you
you always
come back to my mind,
and when you hear me singing
you may know
I am weeping for you.
—NOOTKA LOVE SONG

Blazing cinders Blaise Cendrars for my sake excellence as from a
daughter for my sake uxorious for my sake not dogmatic he
not to be confused with he a father he a gentleman Alice Aurora
Alice allay my fears Alice afterbirth The Star The Victim &
The Poet now there's a theory appointed to be up all
night appurtenance

the Man-Who-Instills Laughter & Tears
talking forever then rolling over talking will take forever then
we'll weep behind closed doors on occasions or rather
occasions such as expanding aging eating pick up & hold the
babies hold them close we'll take forever Alice Albacore
we'll take & steal for that baby we made a movie called
A & B not easy azure it's all over borealis & it's all over
aquamarine tropic so let's call this Daylight & all vote the
social line   We Went Out Laboring

in times of stress—red
for tyrannous authority   & drowning floods, storm, she holds
fire glass jewel red color & blue against wars & enemies, carrying
in the left hand wisdom blades and I give you green,
fears of space so now you know so know you now and don't
turn it around I mean let's use this

I am not grass I can't come to her calling
the waters rise for her I am not water to come for her
wailing forever talking We Went Out Laboring

& everyone & everyone should experience the ease of the
Broadway Ltd   & have a friend who shares adversity distraction
insomnia dreams sigh a white woman sigh hats on hats off
hats on little bright blue towels toast & butter & jam & coffee &
The Inferno the world has oftimes been converted into chaos
are you ready for this? love time & drowning floods,

       flashed out a crimson light I saw a fire which conquered a
hemisphere of darkness
lights & shadow on the page of you I'm reading We write I'm
adding this what dwelt in my dome to those domes and for my
sake howl in jurisprudence

                Bring me my sister

                        she understands
                Bring me my sister, my scribe

                          she is the
                          singer who
                          understands
                          the song
                Bring me my sister

                        she can read visions
                Bring me my sister

                        she understands the
                        heart of the whole
                        matter
bring me my sister I'll tell her all my dreams, wise interpreter
except in cases of shyness, stillness
                bring her to me, bring her me

Albany Buffalo Detroit Chicago   no that wasn't the route.

We're late I get up twice to pee & Valium swallow & climb above
there's no window don't disturb her dissolve into her if at all if all
for my sake, howl, I said howl & beat a drum scratch yr eyes
& lacerate yr mouth   City (Gary) Indiana: LOCK UP!

stacks breathing belching & poison glory color die
I, Lesley, imitate you
You, Frances, time pressure, in this you remind me of
T. M. L. F. B. or B.
a middle name the name of a mother no sex fantasies

I imitate you
the heart of the whole matter
we're on our way, peace of a tranquil
I'm writing this cause we're all gonna die & when we started in
about the record a bruise as dark as chestnut on your breast, me
lacerated if this is poetry I quit No, Man-Who-Instills
Laughter & Tears, I'd never forget you
be reasonable   accumulate dailyness so that the curtain
opens & the sun alights
                    in into brain
& in onto sheet hair body bone   & baby bones

                    make of my bones flutes & whistles, I
implore you in the name of psychological deities female
wrathful & compassionate & protect deer also
Wave Land Dream: Nov. 12. 74:

                         2 Sisters are in the
idyllic town-city tall buildings but always bright blue sky
near water & the light is golden like the Mediterranean & it
reminds me of Greece I was thinking before the
holocaust   glories (rays) raining down on our body-tops
Everyday we go down to the water's edge to get the huge sacks of
mail delivered by the Men-With-No-Eyes-shadows It's always me
the golden who has to dive in to get it The water's

turbulent there's a danger
            must throw my things up to my sister
What's this movie seen this dream before
I throw my coast up to my sister I throw my coat & then I
throw my jewels as if abandonment Always observing my dark
sister from the side half her face is hidden by her hat Long dark
coat & hat pulled down maybe a lady studying the psychology
of mind I think inverted Invertebrates is what we are & we are
mermaids too

        All my dreams here taking place in capital cities like
Lima & Rome & before we even got over to Michigan Avenue
Chicago I've traveled to Mexico City I've never been to Spain
but Bogotá Quito Lima that's enough

                                peace of the tranquil
                                there's a time in this dream
we contemplate & meditate & compare & make observations
We are Scientists we are doctors making a study that's why
we're here. We're from here & we're sent here & a theory
appointed to be up all night apertures

Dear Tequila: I was touchy especially in the bar. I'm sorry.
What can I do? if you knew but you do
                                & there's another theory & movie
The Star:
Needs love, approval, company, money, silence & to go walking
once a day. Buy something. Read scattered hurried the paper
impatient half hour to go perform I'm not actor actress or actrice
no caricature   & it'll only be stale if I'm tired &
empty empty empty fractured   here's a stereo   & here's a
stereo type Likes to be distracted, entertained, gifts jump out of
bed   gets tragic in romance. The apocalypse-spirit inclinations
can't concentrate nothing comes of nothing to a   Transparent
know it all Jive-ass woman

The Victim: Needs love & the intensity of the densest mineral

26

I hesitate: When The World Was Steady

The Victim needs milk the Victim needs ministering to but
the Victim can administrate can talk & carry on be prompt jump
up & make you suffer The Victim is beautiful the victim has eyes
like the dark continent & the raven dark-eyed women
in South America & there are signals & they are the darkest
eyes you ever saw

In the dream it's the Victim & The Star

The Poet is dreaming this

The Poet studies words and makes magic

The Poet stays at home

The Victim ventures out

The Star doesn't stop to think
"I'll have to perform"

Novitiate Road on route to Touchdown Jesus
touchdown Jesus I saw we win
Behind Closed Doors when we get behind closed doors
there's a little one breathing outside & little voice saying open the
door Mommy open the door Daddy
it's not locked it's an illusion of being locked this is an illusion of
journey but it's circular   we are a hit   we win
                              Women-Who-Write-Win Babies

On Nov. 14 in this dream the driver of the Bentley uptown in
Rome gets his arm caught in my Tibetan protection cords his
whole arm has slipped under I can't figure out how &
he's still able to drive and not notice who is this driver?

27

An automaton?   Car full of high-class Mafia thugs we're going
to the big bash uptown, the one with the Pinkerton men in
velvet Rome, Park Avenue, Via Veneto & that place in Mex City
We're hungry & there's going to be no food cause the
automatons don't eat. M. says (he's up front with me):
"Did you see that guy in the back? The blond? That's X's agent!"
He says this very dramatically & sarcastically. X is the driver. As
if an automatic automaton able to drive needed an agent I
wonder X the driver is some kind of writer. What kind of writer?

fast on keys or does he work for the phone company
slow   a mailman fills out forms
deep
lightweight
touchdown
religious
& there are more categories but we ain't interested just so long as
it's words
        signing names to any cause won't but acknowledge
theft out
                it's words I'll have to perform
it's fast speaking
it's klepto
in tongues

I was thinking about that old chanting lady I was thinking
about that old chanting lady & she comes achanting down the
road smoke issuing from her mouth

                        Nov. 14 again

Wake up feel like the world traveler the Star traveler porters &
servants & brandy   more of that, please   a little   like a
cough

smoking at night, beer, you
naming we get dressed up & go out & read words & speak &
give so much we give & it's given back in trust in a trust

save this

A lady Ghostly in a trance like a soft animal being suckled adrift

& I would know how it feels to be sucked
                                        little mouth

little yellow & little pink

                    The Hulk taking me aside thank goodness
& I'm living in this third dream with an Italian family with
revolving doors the thugs guard my privacy, particularly the
entrance of any man   Must always be dressing be redressing
there's glitter & feathers & plenty of makeup & mirrors   They
leave me alone with my rainbow scarf for hours   I'll have to
perform with this scarf

        I have a date—how to escape performing? Get out of this
one Must push through revolving doors like lightning make a
storm or else go out invisibly the scarf making all things invisible
(possibility) Dare to try dare to try little cough

    Treasure Island's food of all nations   When we

passed the Greek section in the dream it was the labels did it

    Swedish mineral water, real Italian pasta

there's so much more
                    eyes on the pool table

We Went Out Laborious
                         I am stabbed with pain   I turn on
the water & it falls the babies never mind   a child
wanders in trance down Broadway & the compassionate
people (ladies) look on   A father   not to be confused with
he a Father   The best   who makes you weep little
silly girl
                    more sons
                         Alice with ambiance

Gary: with S. Hamilton whose dad is X went to school with
Blake in a car: Bristol cream where I've just given a reading on
red carpet leatherbound editions of Virgil & Dante under glass
where I've read for the Catholics & eaten Italian
& talked to students
one who dug rock
one who was the best
one who went to Ireland

The flames & the disasters   the Toll Guards Van Arsdale
shots for the tide 2½ left in the half 7 in the game Averaging
10 points   Center circle   Double Middle   Scott
between.   Someone come up with a basketball my
eyes are tearing NBA air stinging Am. Basketball Assoc.
Nets hot shit   What's his name?

Strong-Man-Along-Side-Mask   Strong-Man-Along-Side-Net

Head Winter-Dancer
                         & we are gowned & grown
& go out on the town   Orsi's
strip joints   you can't get in without a man   Bars
      more beer
Telephone calls

30

"My Heart Belongs to Daddy"   The piano player like Dali
        at the Acorn & Oak

Man-With-A-Mustache   Big-Lady-Who-Sings
        & there are others
& so much more

I imitate you

I nibble

The Sears Tower

The Playboy lunch
                for OUI:
                        concoctions & constellations
& there's always Jupiter & recently there's Jupiter in the sky

I NEVER forget   WE
                Mariner II
I NEVER REPEAT FORGET
I NEVER FORGET   WE
                        corrupting the young & he's so open
& we are the modern ladies, the contemporary women the
women dreaming inside their house!

        barstools   a Chivas for A.   once more
a song   This is a tribe

We fit & we will NEVER NEVER GIVE IT UP

        WOMEN-WHO-WRITE   WOMEN-WHO-SING

& in blood, for my sake & in the name of all you can't explain,
for my sake, in the name of my teeth & nails, for my sake,

Let me try you with my magic power. Let me touch you &
make you whole & perform all the activities of the female
spirit the female Lock-Device from the Dan people or the
people of Zaire & the big cop (I remember these guys from
Chicago in the Sixties, man!) says No Parking. It's the
Lakers & the 49ers & there's no Museum parking today,
day off, sleep til noon, P. comes, our chauffeur. It's been
interesting Yes & we are always interesting & we are always
interesting & we are the most interesting because we are
when the world was steady. We put our masks on & we are
death-connected but it's when the world was steady. We
recognize our fellow female antelope   We romp & flee with
the deer We make of our sweet bones flutes & whistles
          for you to play   You who find us so

Holographs & the voice of Lincoln   "Fourscore and . . .
You who find us Earlier had dinner with Virgil in a dream
he resembled X old College chum of T.C. who became a
Revolutionary
There are more eating scenes—restaurants—then
I have to meet Miguel

          So Sat. morn after Friday on the town a dream in a
restaurant separates tables & singers who sing what you want like
the automatons no food for the singers but a long menu I pick
Retchatoria Wretchatoria or is it Wreckatoria? We are 3,
"spearated" by our style & composure it comes in a tall ice
cream dish—a mixture of pasta with cheese & shirred eggs
I have been wondering about the eggs & think "Sure, they're
eggs" or "Sheer eggs?" or something about stocking nylon etc.
Then it's time, the revolving door again I exit to meet my
better half across a wide Avenue (in the big city again—
there's a square & park like Lima)
I walk out right into the face of an accident—a motorcycle
crushed on its side—someone lifts up a bloody dissevered arm
it's the arm of Marie Antoinette, just a milkmaid—the Victim—

32

here was a warning
I've been warned: WRETCH WRECK   I turn away,
heart pounding hard & solemnly   all joy killed for meeting
those across the Avenue. I walk slowly, they've just emerged
from a classy bus. I'm feeling numb. Miguel says
"After the poker game I took Marlon (Nylon) home with me
& we went to bed." It doesn't hurt.

                    You who find us so
you who find us so   excelling as from daughters sisters
mothers excelling for my sake not to be confused with arrogance
armor we do this in love I mean let's use this like lovers.

1974

From a Continuing Work
in Spanish

1.

I come to you from a dark corner on the farm

I am studying Spanish   *el cielo se oscurece*

yo siento algunas gotas de agua   *es de día*   *buenos días*

es la señorita Spanish, my glance

                              I come to you from Peru

a car crash outside Lima in *The Attempt*

a book without a theme with many events with no person no
                                        personality

except the man who is telling it he's not lying probably

he's very calm

        the wild man with *the studded knife* who weaned the cattle

now kills them mercilessly

                        a bloody mess

a bloody crash

                        South America = blood

it is that time & I am a woman

a woman who dreams of fucking women who fucks women is
                                          not alone is not unusual

a party a dream a party a dream a reunion

              J & M & the novelist is the hotel proprietor.

Whom will I sleep with? who's here now? What is a mammal?

a sticky climate with insects

                    have you heard of the peccary?

& the many marsupials?

                    el sol principia a salir

        2.

I come to you from the woods above Allen's farm there is a view

        at-a-glance   everything moves

                                hace mucho viento

C & I take a walk

                hermano y hermana

              we talk about M & M

        mean & women

        & men who know what they want to do they just do it

women with mammal brain is naturally more just is so live with it
        if you can't

pitch a tent

I come to you from a *big ache*   *acres of land*
          there is no artificial paradise in South America

     tengo mucho que hacer

               la madrugada is the morning

          3.

                    left to itself

I dream a Spanish dream

                    I say "left wing" because it is your grandmother's

     broken life

               listen: start playing

               playing: start, listening

your grandmother is talking but not saying anything.   Her
gray bun

          the Indian woman, black

                    her life on her back

over the mountain

               listen

                    her sharp tongue is not at all like

any bird you could mention

     36

me vuelo

vuelvo

I fly away I go back

I am an ancestor I am big & blond I am a mountain

I am conquistador

viajo

she speaks   she mumbles   she turns

not at all like

any bird you could mention

4.

not a way to go.   **an ocean.**   a lake.   a
raging river.

the narrows

Someone is hungry

the children are hungry   they don't look like you

we are related but we are also related to the big dog and to the
dino dinosaur

con ella no pueden igualarse

los tesoros que la tierra

contiene ni el mar encubre

with to can not be compared the treasures which the earth

contains or

    sea

      hides

          a woman is *mi madre*

       solo solo

    5.

sweating)

      my lover's arm touches the sky

      it's a sacred land between rock & river

      sweet   lazy   watery   blue

          he's so high

      means: temper with a plan

      means: of course

      means: I've taken my chances

         not sorry

         not going back

he's got arms of steel

he's got a cock of steel

come, my sisters, & play with his long dark hair

6.

the lover

    the hand that feeds the mother

the dogs barking

    the guitar

        no lo entiendo

I come I conquer

          start playing

      listen: temper with a plan

a woman who dreams of fucking women who fucks women is
                  not alone is not unusual

     a bloody mess

      South America equals blood

   sweet lazy watery blue

           restless dogs shaking collars in

             half-sleep

   ni el mar encubre

       hombre y mujer

   brother & sister

the novelist a hotel proprietor

amor

woman who dreams of

fucking

at a glance

everything moves

I come to you

tengo mucho que hacer

nada nada

whom will I sleep with?   Who's here now?   what is a mammal?

7.

A sacred land between rock & river

restless dogs

gas lamps

fantastic storm

people turning in their old beds

big people mumbling & moving about

night birds

the wild man with *the studded knife* who weaned the cattle

now kills them mercilessly

hace claro de luna

know Spanish

put it in your mouth & roll it around

la cama means bed

where I go

& wait

esperemos

fíjese el plan, gracias

8.

I go I conquer I wake up

there is no artificial paradise in South America

a party a dream a reunion

mapping

a woman a mother a grandmother a lover

I wait   I write   I travel

I come to you from a dark corner on the farm

I come to you from Peru

41

climb by train

return by plane

       I come to you from a dark corner on the farm

I wait   I start   I stop

   my lover sleeps in the attic

big people stumble & move about

                   gas lamps

                   fantastic storm

know passion

    know Spanish

  a city built by conquistadors is never modest, never

        dreaming

 a woman, her life on her back

stoops

   not at all like any bird you could mention

   9.

        el mar encubre

  solo solo

above Allen's farm there is a view & everything moves

men & women

take a walk

there is no paradise in North America

I write from a dark corner

in peace & quiet

my life on my back

I read & study

a book without a theme with many events

with no person no personality

whom will I sleep with?   who's right here?   what is the country?

South America = blood

la madrugada is the morning

acres of land

I dream a Spanish dream

tempered with a plan

10.

the mother   takes the lover

she mumbles   she turns

a dog jumps on *la cama*

the man who weaned the cattle he's very calm

a man with no themes no personality

over the mountain

night birds

not a way to go.

have you heard of the peccary & the many marsupials?

her sharp tongue

it's a sacred land between rock & river

listen   listen   listen

a woman who dreams of fucking women who fucks women is
not unusual

is not alone

her master, the life on her back

her black hair, the only home you can mention

los tesoros que la tierra contiene

my lover sleeps above

someone is hungry

everything moves

restless dogs shake their collars in half-sleep

11.

            a lake   a raging

an ocean

        narrows

                we are related to the big dog

& the dinosaur

                awake the *"noticias"*

a Latin beat, do you remember?

                do you remember grandmother like a mountain

                heaving?

                                        wild?

    con ella no pueden igualarse

ni el mar encubre

                                        conquistador

        ancestor

            crash

                        I come to you from a big ache

left to itself

                tengo mucho que hacer

12.

esperemos

    mapping

        mountains & a city shrouded in fog

mountains & a lover upstairs

        he's very calm

           not sleeping probably

learn   grow

      climb by plane

a city built by conquerors is never modest, never dreaming

      I dream a Latin dream

      I dream a poet's dream

      el cielo se oscurece

      a sticky climate with insects

men & women

      woman with mammal brain

      man with arms of steel

      hermano y hermana

13.

with many events with no person no personality

where am I?   with whom will I sleep?

she speaks   she turns

what is the country?

mi madre

la madrugada

it's that time

who dreams of fucking

night birds

a modern dream

14.

a country so big where is its mother?

I come to you from

studying passion

with to cannot be compared the treasures

which the earth contains or sea hides

a bloody mess

the radio blaring the *noticias*

hombre y mujer

come, my sisters, &

stumble in the dark

15.

solo solo

the wild man with the studded knife who weaned

the cattle now kills them mercilessly

this is a mother-book

me vuelo

this is dark-continent-time

I write to you from a corner on the farm

it's dangerous

There is no artificial paradise in South America.

Shaman Hisses You Slide Back into the Night

The Rolling Thunder Revue *with Bob Dylan at its center was a notable phenomenon, a moving body of artistic individuals, traveling somewhat spontaneously from place to place to perform, interact, and make a movie. I was hired on—with Allen Ginsberg—as a kind of poet-in-residence-witness to contribute ideas to and make a brief appearance in what was to become the epic-length film* Renaldo & Clara. *The public shows were but one aspect, and a powerful one. Dylan on stage in white face, a feather in his hat, mouthing the syllables, surrounded by a host of impressive musicians and guest stars, was catalyst, energy-principle, the word-worker, and "technician of the sacred," i.e., shaman. This poem came out of a journal of the trip and includes a litany-homage to Dylan, overheard phrases, dreams, places, extrapolations, and other humming informations. We were a peripatetic tribe, a merry band of gypsies and a rock 'n' roll show. It was a precious time, hard to capture, quintessentially American, a paradigm perhaps of how we'd all like to live—**on the road,** the poet's utopia.*

it turns me weak it turns me weak   it turns me weak

invocation

    against that hunger may I roam
    at twilight may I roam
    when the night is splendidly lit may I roam

    against shaman's shadow may I roam
    against the power may I roam
    against the synthesizer may I roam

       & for a glimpse may I roam
       & make you smile

This is something about power taking off its clothes & laboring
     & at the moment I did not know the value of knowledge
to make sore by friction

       Observe the structure of a group, each flickering detail
surrounding shaman

    this one lights, this one drives, this one makes you laugh,
this one drums, that one's purely Byzantine
                there's The Woman-Who-Manages
The Woman-Who-Sets-Up, The Money-Man, the Advance-Man
       The Man-Who-Collects-the-Bags

nothing to do with meliorism

or custodians

nothing to do with foxholes nothing to do with commandos or
cursory remarks nothing to do with palaver everything
to do with public space everything to do with private glimpse

            nothing to do with punctuation.   Trucks.
Little Dot Beauty Shop. Crossing the Housatonic in the rain with
   playwright Sam.
Dash all hope.   Nothing to do with Sam.

      o my wasted eyes looking so hard
    staying up studying myself

something about the wandering woman, Muslim, one cloth wound
   about another

headdress   something about Braille

50

something about Egypt. Hierarchy. Germany. Reason pales &
    needing
no approval or veneration the way a King might   something about
                stampede

                & performing
                & duty

THE TECHNICIANS SHOW US THEIR GAPING MOUTHS   A moving
    kingdom . . .

& clearly the pressure makes its imprint on the body turning me weak
it turns me weak it turns me weak it turns me weak
                it turns me weak

        ♦

I write to pass the time   Solo. Midnight. I spy the source

I am the frequent bystander.   Molecular

                A man-woman   A woman-man   a shaman

a man who makes a song to heal

                        Elegance

        coercion

                        diffidence

                Danbury, Connecticut, at the beginning

I ask for Dr. William Carlos Williams at the desk (Ginsberg's alias)
shirk all duty and keep the memory of the heart

        Vicissitudes & finally, to vocalize

◆

& shaman he swings a skinny leg to the sky
& shaman he desires you be there watching
shaman don't care about eating now
he's got his paint on he's ready for jive
& shaman's going to sway & gesture in space
& shaman's shouting yeah for you
& singing your sorrow
shaman's not faithful except to you
shaman does it for you   you know all this
shaman's got his eyes on the violin
shaman's moving his eyeballs around
shaman's in Rome
shaman's going to finish what he started
shaman grows old & never changes
O shaman leave your dog outside!
shaman makes no mistake
shaman lights a Gitane
shaman hisses you slide back into the night
shaman makes you disappear
cuts you out to include you
shaman's pacing   & clocks your confusion
shaman makes you hungry to feed you
shaman in black & white
shaman a walking, talking kachina doll
shaman around five feet tall
shaman struts
shaman's brim casts a shadow
shaman points a toe
shaman wears a feather
shaman is reckless
shaman in whiteface
shaman barks a meter
shaman speaks occasionally
shaman dedicates this one to the great American writer
shaman appears on the right

shaman boots a compadre
shaman takes you west
shaman cuts the brush
shaman yawns & gazes out window
shaman gets gruff for you
       reaches the high notes
       has a family
       eats turkey
       swings his guitar like a baby
       is a baby
       is sometimes a woman
       is casting off
       centripetal force
shaman drives a hard bargain
shaman mixes it up
shaman is obvious o shaman so obvious
shaman won't be there
shaman takes liberties
shaman touches the ocean
shaman don't drown
shaman echoes himself
shaman bites down hard on the wind
you'd better well listen to shaman
shaman takes abuse
shaman don't mind
shaman takes pains
shaman knows the song
shaman's fingers are smaller than mine
BUT SHAMAN HAS A THOUSAND FINGERS!
shaman don't ride airplanes
shaman is flying you home
shaman provides
shaman depends on you
shaman leaves it open
shaman is surrounded
shaman brushes a hand through his hair
shaman wears no wig

shaman wears a garden on his head
shaman is a faun
shaman mediates
shaman is modern
shaman is medieval
shaman don't meddle
shaman is almost Chinese
shaman likes the cold
shaman is a harbor
shaman breathes across metal reeds
shaman makes you cleave to rocks
shaman blows you away
you'd better well go away
shaman heeds the percussion
shaman slows down
shaman dedicates this one to Brigham Young
shaman snaps another string
shaman's heels wear down
but shaman has timbrels in his voice
shaman has an ocean in his voice
shaman has a mean man in his voice
shaman has a chromium lover in his voice
shaman has disaster in his voice
shaman has all the creatures & especially a jaguar in his voice
shaman has carpets in his voice
shaman has icicles in his voice
shaman has pleasure in his voice
shaman types the paragraphs in his voice
shaman leaves no ordinary trace
shaman imprinting on you
shaman is a victim for you
shaman is vagrant for you
shaman vindicates you
shaman is vigorous
shaman rides a horse
shaman loves a goddess
shaman says his thoughts vanish before they come

shaman still wandering
shaman lost his shadow
shaman don't need a shadow
shaman's shadow is scattered & walked upon
in this dream:

MURDER OF PASOLINI DREAM: NOVEMBER 7

A big photo-realism movie called »Written on the Wind« is being made
in Rome, aggressive color & behavior. A war between the races—the
Reds & the Blues. They're all men and I'm androgynous »reporter«.
Pasolini very abstract, behind his lens in black jumpsuit. Protestors (the
Blues) with huge banners reading »UP AGAINST A WALL, ROMA«
and »UP AGAINST WALL, AROMA« and »WALL AMOR«. A gang of
armored youngsters (sons of the Reds) with machine guns (like Bur-
roughs's Wild Boys) break in on the shooting of movie, force us into
large department store in which we're forced to take poses in the store
windows like mannequins. Then we're all lined up to be shot.
I remember thinking he's »a lean one« of Pasolini. He's got aviator's
goggles & cigarette dangling from his mouth & bows his head as the
Red Boys take aim.

NAVIGATING THE DREAM

Avoid further meditation but not because it might be harmful
what is harmful or not harmful nothing to do with the question
Rather consider the river rising grows mightier & nourishes the soil
maintaining its own course until it reaches the sea all the more
   welcome ally
You may urge your meditations on the decrees of shaman
Thus far you may not urge your meditation on the decrees of shaman
My inquiry is purely historical   no lightning flashes any longer from
the long since vanished thunderclouds so I may venture no people
can menace us here   The artists show us their gaping mouths and
this tribe moves from place to place   We sing for the invaders
We have not seen them & if we remain in these moving villages we
shall never see them if on their wild horses they should ride as

hard as they could straight toward us   We are always disappearing
and the land is vast   they end their course in empty air
That is the frustration of the people who follow
We tempt them to be at the mercy of shaman
Why did we leave our homes our weeping husbands
& wives   children that need care and depart for strange towns &
highways while our thoughts stayed on them
This is a question for shaman
The leader knows us though absorbed in giant anxieties   knows our
petty pursuits   The high command has existed from ancient time like
a gathering of elders summoned hastily to discuss someone's fine dream
drummed out of their beds before dawn
The illuminations die down but I won't hold my tongue
The most obscure of our institutions is shaman   Except
for our holidays & rituals filling the whole year we think
only on shaman   One hears a great many things but one gathers
nothing definite   I dig my little room   So vast is the land
nothing does justice to the vastness   But he is mighty throughout
the hierarchies of the land   He a human like us lies on his couch
of generous proportions
Like us he stretches & when he is tired, yawns
We think only of him of whom we know little   how true is the
curiosity that fills us   We are always trying to get information
on shaman but strange as it sounds it is almost impossible
to discover anything even from those who have wandered
though they navigate our little dream & river

> And one day he sends a message to you the humble subject
> the insignificant shadow cowering in the modest distance

> He has sent it to you alone whispered to a trusted messenger
> But the multitudes are so vast the numbers have no end

> ♦

shaman I had this dream the other night me & two red men were
decorating each other's backs with faces & suddenly I realized you
   could paint the front too & I thought heh
we gotta tell this to shaman

56

♦

shaman's a clever animal who might also be human
shaman's making you nervous
shaman: is it natural?
shaman the world's bleeding for ya
heh shaman, slip into this
shaman the night's barely old enough
shaman you ain't so elegant
shaman git back in your element
shaman don't embarrass us
shaman is emaciated
shaman is eloquent
shaman your diction's so good
shaman you remind me of the lone wapiti
shaman's so surly

heh shaman what about chemistry
are people really what they seem?

shaman may I ask another question?
heh shaman what about it heh

shaman expose more hypocrisy
shaman tell us the ball scores
shaman take it into the daylight
shaman please snarl for us
shaman you know about dalliance?
shaman you a ladies' man?
shaman holds the door open then shaman darts away

then I had this other dream shaman you were on the telephone
saying Tell it to Brazil

shaman you think New York City's all about economy?

I guess you're right
shaman hypnotize us
shaman deactivate us

shaman you're putting us in a deadlock is that what you want?
shaman everybody's talking about you
shaman everybody's writing about you
I can't get away from you shaman

I go all the way to South Carolina & I gotta hear about shaman
cause you got here first

shaman unshackle us
shaman what are my defects?
shaman you'll never be didactic
shaman speak to us, say something
don't be standoffish
you're so brisk, shaman
shaman you think the skin's simply a veneer?
shaman wields the power
shaman now they're complaining about you
shaman they're out to get you
they say you have too much money but shaman I don't mind
shaman you're wily
there's a sham in shaman

♦

»We shamans in the interior have no special spirit language and
believe that the real *angatkut* do not need it. On my travels I have
sometimes been present at a séance among the saltwater Dwellers.
These *angatkut* never seemed trustworthy to me. It always appeared to
me that these saltwater *angatkut* attached more weight to tricks that
would astonish the audience, when they jumped about the floor and
lisped all sorts of absurdities and lies in their so-called spirit language;
to me all this seemed only amusing and as something that would im-
press the ignorant. A real shaman does not jump about the floor and

do tricks, nor does he seek by the aid of darkness, by putting out lamps, to make the minds of his neighbors uneasy. For myself, I do not think I know much, but I do not think that wisdom or knowledge about things that are hidden can be sought in that manner. True wisdom is only to be found far away from people, out in the great solitude, and is not found in play but only through suffering. Solitude and suffering open the human mind, and therefore a shaman must seek his wisdom there.«

—Igjugarjuk
Caribou Eskimo

POEM

love grows   finds that's only
the beginning
he'll fly across to play
pulls at his sleeve   I try to live
he says
the public
isn't a bystander will marvel
heroes more colorful
I sing right to myself to millions
a personal theory
zest is infectious
& tenderness is publicity
everything from perfume, makeup
1 stage suits & suites
have them do this flat seaming
on my shoulders
he beams
to have an audience is hazardous
»they turn me weak«
head right for books
& appalled by the frenzy
of our days
limousines give me a rise
why do musicians quiver like aspic?

lineage of a golden throat
home was a green & growing place
begins in Nashville, Tennessee

JOURNAL:

Ethan Allen would have loved this Inn
»They're in there, rehearsing.«
»Jim, will you guide her in?«

»Yeah.   What about Van Gogh?«
as I enter the room

November 11

jamming

this is about some kind of agreement that doesn't have to work
you sit down & there you go there you go
you take a solemn seat
a room with no personality
except the music
something to drink, please
everybody waiting on shaman
He lights my Gitane   it breaks up   talking about Amiri Baraka now
& Neuwirth singing a touching song
»don't fall down«
for the highwire artist
&
»Please tell Allen Ginsberg to lighten up about the coke.«
(Roger grinning)

a man's medley is reaping a benefit   man is medley-prone
twofold   having two layers   composed of two of the same kind
composed of 2 different kinds   twice as much   designed for 2
twofold   in a pair   twice the quantity   twice the fold

a duplicate & not a double boiler or potboiler so I suspect
                (always the sense of a wide-eyed woman)
indefatigable
                        Scarlet-The-Shadowy-Who-Saws-Strings (a musician)
        & Gelsey's sister horsing in the halls
& Madonna kicking her legs in the air   lets out a scream
            romping in the corridors
                fatigue
                    more music
& conversing on the clean lines of Dr. William Carlos Williams

        Allen tossing & turning the night away
I sit inside the dawn
& now I lay me down in motel slumber

            ◆

Niagara Falls I tell Allen about thunder myth & how it hurts
we write poem for rock musicians' newsletter & they are suspicious
of a clever woman
so it's strictly thunder & brandy
& singing when we listen
turned & tuned in upon themselves
it's the boyhood I like & confidence
& I do not place anything on top of this unit
I dream a writer's dream & Pasolini's murder
O the streets of Rome!
arms swinging
always the fault of a competent man
so this is what's happening:
no one to talk to but film crew & I have to talk
it's always talk
it's before I got born

so
it's this
& this is a memory:
many hours through blizzard I stared out super bus Phydeaux

saw Joni's musical fire & caught the air
I wish this in memorable space for the time we spent
we a tribe   no threat   love & assurance
this is not a lament only occasionally when it's lonely

I dream   a man dancing under tremendous rain clouds
I bolt awake in Niagara Hilton ready to face the music
spread it around
a movie gets made   Boston, Connecticut, Maine, Canada

◆

POEM: COCAINE

. . . .
            leisure
            Inca
                  (drawl)
            droll
            positron
            libertine (male or female)

ligneous
escudo
                  INVINCIBLE!

I am absolutely positively certain!

Pepin the Short, King of the Franks
            father of Charlemagne dies AD 768

      deflection (as in swerve)
      tacks
      tact
            clemency
            clench
            muscles
            eyeballs

62

THE EYE IS A MUSCLE!

multiple twin instrument of vision . . .

NIJINSKY DREAM: NOVEMBER 13

»The little horse is tired« he says folding his soft pink calf dancing shoes
into a matchbox. »I have the matchbox blues.« The audience descends
upon him, he goes and puts his face to the wall and makes as if running
with his bare feet that seem red and sore.

Dear Douglas:

I tell you this it's about no one falling in love exactly it's
about falling in love in another country

the tribe is loyal

tall buildings
          a plaza
or else the rail of a boat   it's simple no it's easy
no it's a wooden rail with brass trim   that's what   see?
or drenched in desert light you know the way the landscape turns
me weak
it turns me weak   it turns me weak   it turns me weak
a lamp is necessary   now a lamp is totally necessary   so this is about
some kind of travel
          in dreams in buses

                    we bus here we bus there
we are stopping
          life is always a bust
                    to cross a border

after Thanksgiving
all these men look like Kerouac and about the age when he died
but frozen here in time & space but hanging in there in time &
speaking a kind of *patois* on the outskirts of winter's magic power
fall on my ears & kiss the snow
.& this is the truth
café avec sucre   *café au lait*
winter's magic powder

Saturday November 29 in the early a.m. Quebec City
run in snow expanding to river
la rivière

(the world's biggest necklace)
the cameras rolling
& we can walk around here unlike the freeways
& »I like the north«
»isn't this something?«
Château Frontenac
front & back   neck & back
I like the way I have to keep looking for everything & everyone
& dig my little room
red velvet curtains
red walls
we shoot the »brothel scene«
women in bras and boas
»Renaldo, where is Clara?«

Dear Douglas:
*après la conquête les Canadiens purent conserver leur langue
et leur coutumes Aujourd'hui . . .*
les rues étroites héroïques et historiques
fondée par Samuel de Champlain
in the name of France
& in the name of England *vaincu le Général
Montcalm*

sur les plaines d'Abraham

sur les plaines d'Abraham

♦

shaman get to bed don't tarry
shaman let's have a miracle
shaman we made for each other?
shaman has it gotta be?
shaman take your hat off
shaman take your necklace off
shaman your mother is talking to you
shaman get behind the wheel
shaman take your watch off
shaman you're showing more interest than anyone
shaman you're tantamount to King
shaman tap your legs again
shaman stop tantalizing us
shaman you're a mischief maker
monkey shaman
shaman give me a souvenir don't yawn
impious shaman
it's implicit shaman
Elizabethan shaman
primitive shaman
no tryst shaman
camaraderie
tropology
& shaman you're too much you're making me pick up the tab
but
shaman's lady is lovely
shaman's lady adorns her body
shaman's lady is wise
shaman's lady sleeps on a bed of twigs
I'll give my words to shaman's lady
& she'll take them down the triple highway

so that

at night may I roam
against the winds may I roam
at night may I roam
when the owl is hooting may I roam

at dawn may I roam
against the winds may I roam
at dawn may I roam
when the first bird is calling may I roam

& into the heart may I roam
& against the dazzle may I roam
& for the music may I roam
when the tribe is calling may I roam

& gaping wide may I roam
& gaping wide may I roam

CODA: THE EAGLE & THE MOON GODDESS

for Sarah

The eagle lives under the sky far above us
He's so beautiful
In his talons he holds his world
He wears a gay garment, a vibrant moist coat of colors
He waits there for the words of the Moon Goddess
Bright-eyed he looks down upon his world
His eyes are turned towards the West
Bright-eyed he looks down upon the waters of life
His eyes radiate calamity
The sun is bright & magnificent in his eyes

His feet are red
He spreads his wings wide over the earth
& beneath his wings the gods grant rain the gods grant dew
Dew comes forth on the planet
His voice rises above us
Lovely are the words
Even the Moon Goddess hears them
She who lives in the underworld
She hears them there & responds
The words of the Moon Goddess mingle with the words of the eagle
The words of the eagle fade & drift above the waters

The words of the Goddess drift
underneath the sky dome

Far away their words vanish

— Cora Indian Song

DECEMBER

John Cage & Merce Cunningham are performing in a corridor in blue workshirts. I dream their gestures, like seaweed. John has a wand-twig which he attempts to plant on my head & I'm worried about not having enough »soil« up there. He then pats me soothingly and gives his marvelous great big glee laugh! Something about »just keep it watered.« Dylan comes to call and is made a bit nervous by these gents, they are taller than he is. But everyone is polite and it is understood that Dylan will collaborate and learn to dance by observing their gestures. I say to him »You ought to write a song about Nijinsky«.

Dream interrupted by phone ringing—it's Dylan! I'm staying at dance loft of Douglas Dunn on Broadway & Dylan is in the neighborhood & will come to call. He brings as a gift the big gold Nijinsky book with splendid photographs.

Allen Ginsberg & I go visit Dylan who's living in a series of cabins on a lake on the Lower East Side. He's seemingly in a dark mood for as we enter we find him attempting to climb into his guitar case like a coffin. Soothed by our sudden appearance he gestures toward some color Polaroid snapshots of his kids taken in the woods, which are balancing on the arm of a plush stuffed forest-green chair. We ask him about his work—his »book«—& he throws back a gruff laugh. As we go to let in more visitors including Clark Coolidge, Gregory Corso, and a girl desk clerk from the Hotel Boulderado, Dylan slips into one of the back cabins.

I take a walk in the woods and have a pearly white dagger handle thrown at me (which I catch) by a guy named »Don« who's standing on an embankment. He explains it is the »speciality of these woods«. Then he throws an entire dagger which stabs the ground at my feet & starts the whole place on fire.

Gregory & I have an interchange as the fire is raging. He comments that my leather pants are »4 feet too long«.

Everyone is frantic now trying to rescue books and papers & Bob himself who has locked himself into another one of the back cabins which is now in flames. I break the glass in the window & wake up.

mingle	calamity	moist	coda	gaping	adorns
tab	camaraderie	tantamount	gotta	leur	après
freeways	November	powder	patois	bust	weak
drenched	brass	loyal	Douglas	Connecticut	rain
lament	memorable	Phydeaux	Rome	Pasolini	unit
brandy	rock	Niagara	fatigue	indefatigable	prone
Roger	Gitane	seat	Ethan	Journal	shaman
wily	didatic	unshackle	away	deadlock	economy
Brazil	dream	dalliance	scores	chemistry	surly
diction	bleeding	clever	paint	red	multitudes
shadow	humble	river	shaman	yawns	holidays

obscure   tongue   die   ancient   children   horses
moving   tribe   gaping   decrees   urge   ally
river   further   navigating   shadow   imprinting   you
paragraphs   jaguar   chromium   timbrels   snaps   down
cleave   harbor   Chinese   modern   faun   wig
thousand   pains   shaman   ocean   obvious   centripetal
baby   guitar   gruff   compadre   American   meter
feather   brim   struts   kachina   hungry   clocks
Gitane   Rome   eyeballs   gesture   jive   sky
vocalize   vicissitudes   Danbury   coercion   bystander
gaping   kingdom   Egypt   Braille   Dot   meliorism
Byzantine   shaman   flickering   friction   moment   This

a man-woman a shaman a man who makes a song to heal
a woman-man a sha-man a woman makes this song to heal
a mannerism a shaman has a man who plays a drum to heal
a woman singing a woman dancing a woman makes a place a meal
a spinning man a clay man a shaman takes your song for fuel
a watching woman-man a shaman watches & plans a song to make
    you well
a showman makes a song so smart to heal it swell
a woman-man a he-she man takes this place to steal the show
a man-woman a shaman woman makes the song appeal
steel man inside shaman gesture in blue
salmon color woman skin make her skin a drum to heal

                                        1976

Our Past

You said my life was meant to run from yours as
     streams from the river.
You are the ocean I won't run to you
We were standing on Arapahoe in front of the Silver
     Saddle Motel
They had no rooms for us
I wore the high red huaraches of Mexico & a long skirt
     of patches
You had traveled back from Utah
I thought of the Salt Lakes, seeing them once from a
     plane they were like blank patches in the mind or
     bandaged places of the heart
I felt chilly
I had just ridden down the mountain with a car full of
     poets, one terrified of the shifting heights, the
     dark, the mountains, he said, closing in
I said Wait for me, but I have to go here first, or, it's too
     complicated, some kind of stalling because I
     wanted you
You were direct, you were traveling light, your feet
     were light, your hair was light, you were attentive
Were you rushing me?
We walked by the stream, you held me, I said I have to
     get back soon because he's waiting, maybe he's
     suffering
I think the moon was waning
You walked me back along 9th Street under dark trees
The night we'd met, June 6, we'd come out of the New
     York Church to observe a performer jumping over
     signposts
I was with my friend, a mentor, much older
You were introduced to him, to me
You said you'd followed me out from that night to where
     the continent divides, where my heart divided

I wrote poems to you in Santa Fe
You followed me all the way to Kitkitdizze
I waited for you, when you came I was away
I drove miles to speak with you on the telephone
I met you in Nevada City after nearly turning back to
      put out a fire
We went to Alta, the lake of your childhood
I wanted to stay forever in the big room with all the
      little white beds, like a nursery
You were like first love
All the impossibilities were upon us
We never had enough time
In Palo Alto where they name the streets after poets I
      admired your mother's pretty oriental things
In San Francisco we ate hurriedly at the joint near the opera house
I lied about going to Chicago for your birthday in New York
I lied about spending Christmas with you in Cherry Valley
I will never forget the dance you did to the pipes of
      Finbar Furey on New Year's Day. You kept your
      torso bent to protect your heart
Then I moved to Colorado
We met and sat in the yard of a friend's brother's house in
      Missoula, Montana
It's wonderful the way this city turns serenely into
      country with no fuss, the city is shed, or is it the
      other way around, the country falls off into the city?
It was how I wanted us to shed our other lives at least
      when we were together
In that yard you made me feel our situation was
      intolerable
We seemed to be in constant pain
When we parted at the small airport early that morning
      my heart finally ripped
In the spring back in New York, things got darker
I was sick, my head was swollen
I remember reading to you about the Abidharma on a mattress
I had trouble speaking

I behaved badly and embarrassed you at the uptown
     party
A part of you had left me for good
You'd given your loft over to weekly parties
You were having a public life. I felt you were turning
     into me
I wanted our private romance
Was I being straight with you, I wondered?
I let you think things of me that weren't true. You
     thought I was wise & couldn't be hurt
          Then I had the person I lived with and what could
          be said about that?
That summer you visited my hotel in Boulder. We
     slept on separate mattresses. I felt I was trying to
     imprison you and after you left I couldn't go back
     there for days. When I did I found a dead bird had
     gotten entrapped, struggled fiercely to get out
The following winter I waited for you in subzero cold,
     wearing black. I was told you'd come & gone. You
     didn't return. We spoke on the phone a long time
I said I was going home and falling in love with someone
     else. You said It sounds like you want to
My mother heard me crying and came to me in the
     bathtub and said O don't, it breaks my heart! I
     told her I was going to the hell for a while I'd often
     made for others, karma works that way. Bosh
     karma she said
We've met briefly in Portland, Oregon, and New York
We've corresponded all this time, following the details
     of each other's lives and work
Your father has recently died
My baby son grows stronger
The last time I saw you you were standing on my
     street corner
As I came toward you you said What a youthful gait
     you have

Travel Being Love

I awoke in an ancient country to you
You smelled of lilac, of musky dew
& tasted of salt & sex
I heard you moan like a beast
The arrangement of your limbs was intense
I was reading the life of a dead poet
You pretended to be asleep, ha!
The bracelet on your arm over your face
hid a blue eye
I saw you quiver & expect something
I smelled your lemony hair
I heard a far car swish like a fish
& someone yell "Frankie!"
I heard the motor hour go by
Then caught myself touching you again
You didn't want any words or places
where we hadn't yet met
Managua? Sri Lanka? Halifax?
Listen: We sat later in the Black Rose
near the Aquarium
where an Irish lilt filled the air
Sweet guys & girls off boats
at the next table were drinking & smoking
You said "Vrindaban!" and "Life's a switch"

These lines are swift returns
I smelled that you had been hiding many years
& invited you again to this restaurant
where the blinds clatter
The light shifts
A man coughs loudly
Your face hesitates on the border between us
While a green oilcloth shines in a new light.

Nomad's Song

the scene of my selves, the occasion of these ruses
—FRANK O'HARA

I meet my selves when we cry like water
Two halves deepen to a pact
where ambitious chromosomes mix
and "matter" as habit goes napping
for matter resists the will to sing
Materialism is a scourge for the nomad

You carry your life nomadically
and search the desert for water
Find the sylvan source, you sing
and make a nature-pact
It's time long past napping
Get up! The *carpe diem* reviews are mixed

Water is rising over some book I'm mixed
up about, wrenched from context, not a nomad
although mirages are here after napping
a veritable flood, and contamination—worry of water
all dark dealings and pacts
You name it: business, government, How to sing

above them? Won't do simply to sing
The complaynt is poem of tainted mix
of timbres, the complaynt is a pact
with yourself to always harbor the nomad
inside you who seeks fresh water
and resists dominion, no napping

in sinews, in secret heart: no napping
in sinews, in secret heart: more singing

74

in sinews, in heart that hides: water metaphors
in sinews, love the mix
in sinews and marrow: the sinewy nomad
With the whole body, a sacred pact

Be true to the cellular pact
when cells to cells oppose napping
and leave a mind free of matter, nomadic
It wanders, it wanders, singing
and always dancing a kind of mischief
calmed by sustenance of water

Water is life, equiposed to a pact
mixed in you 100 percent naturally
and you sing, your selves liberated as a nomad

Blue Mosque

to William S. Burroughs

This is many lifetimes from the capital of India speaking. I've been out of the Muslim world now 24 hours. I've just come from Gate 4 North Block Ministry of Home Affairs. All is ok on the corners of Parliament House and President House. Tawny monkeys are lining the roof walk. They seem to be laughing. Please note I'm leaving my passport No. J193934 at the Nepalese Embassy Baracamba Road overnight after some tears with the guys from Royal Nepali Airlines. They are competing with Air India for my ticket money. I am not what I seem, tourist in pink-stripe shirt, gold chain, gray cloth paths, rope soles from Italy. I am not what he wants, dark Hindu works for Universal Tires and has lived in Tehran. Terror ran. He is always waiting for me on Connaught Circle. "Don't cry, Anne," he says, tapping me lightly on the shoulder, "they are ok. But you must have a cool drink." I am not all's fine with work & life PS Love. I am not enabling to get me to Darjeeling today, thank you Madam. I am not Dianne Vanderlip. I am no student discount rates please. Traveler de Luxe Olympia $150 American how many rials. Where is rials? River of laws.

Please note I am not old woman birthday April 2 still a flowing river cause you cross me, D. Peter dark Hindu will not be dining with the Madam Anne tonight. Her husband is joining her. This is not the truth this is sorta truth in rupees. Woodlands Vegetarian Restaurant I attended with the authors Giorno and Brownstein October 1973 is, I am happy to report, still standing. Mr. Jain and Mrs. Colaco on Janpath Lane are receiving guests in their hotel. This prose was speaking of Capital Delhi note leaving the Muslim world this is Ascendant Leo 4 degrees speaking.

"CABLE BLUE MOSQUE"

Leaving the Muslim world I was always watching them under their

76

cloths and some, at airport, with platform shoes shocking pink, plastic Mediterranean blue pants with red makeup. Paula with blond widow's peak of England says some woman got acid thrown in her face for baring her face. There are hints and murmurs from all quarters. Never go bare face in that bazaar. The star People personalities of the Shah and his wife and their son with their big faces plastered everywhere and through Tabriz the scent of blood. On the Mihan bus: he loves me well, he keeps me down. Where are they putting those bodies in the Biblical landscape ah weeping my Gideon. I will go down to the Caspian Sea. I will weep for the daughters of Jordan and Zion and the little Marxist children.

And before that and before that and before that and before that and before that and before that and before that. I am not what I seem leaving the western world, boarding again the Orient Express in Bulgaria green corduroy pants, green sweater, black shawl, very cold in the morning. He grabbed my tits in Tabriz. I am not what I am doing. So the coal strike has ended at last Monday March 27. There are hints and murmurs from all quarters that the major issues have not been resolved and you will notice no one is claiming a triumph, no one. Make a note: It started with the original strategic mistake (paper ripped here) for rude and (continues fragmented) the internal cha-Taft Hartley procedure successful on a dubious sense that amatory instant negotiators on the went back to work etc. But a tunate precedent has been hangin unencable and ignored energy ago extremely rap coal produc in Appalach contact the epidemics . . . . "Jimmy" OK.

OK Blue Mosque. "CABLE BLUE MOSQUE"

This is whew from the capital of India where no man is molesting me during Prohibition. I forgot my little paper at the airport, paper says that I out of all these millions may have a spirit drink. I was so hungry so thirsty leaving the Muslim world these women coming at me in their black shrouds with their eyes on me their eyes of lust for not taking the shroud off keeping the shroud on reminds me of a friend of my mother's (this is somewhere in the Thirties) who would go around naked in her fur coat and expose herself in expensive restaurants. Was thinking of the lewd men of the Muslim world and their past beauty putting eyes on me. He grabs me in Tabriz. Another on Sizdeh Bedar April 2 my birthday wrings my hand. Then another touches my thigh ever so subtly. This is the day 13 days after the new year when it's unlucky to stay inside until after sunset. My lover and I make love in the Arm Strong Hotel, collapse into separate beds until sunset, go out braving the Muslim world.

I am not what I seem. I leave him on the corner of Ferdowski near the buses to Mashhad. I get in an orange taxi with a flat tire. Then a German enters the car and says "It is yours, Madam" 150 rials away from the airport from the lover 10 kilometers to the airport. Please note I am traveling alone visa here good till August. My No. is J193934 I have no passport for 12 hours please note if you are getting this wire. OK

BLUE MOSQUE OK

And after that and after that and after that and after that and after that and after that and after that and after that there's a little man from Malaysia who takes pity on me I am very hungry I am very thirsty he is western medicine man assures me there's sure to be a "snatch" on the plane. Then he buys me a beer (my last for 2 months) and miraculously produces a sandwich from a paper bag. My hotel stationery says "Cable: Manhood." Going on in a Muslim world.

OK BLUE MOSQUE

Then 2 Armenians one born in Russia find us on Pahlavi Avenue after eating the best chicken kebob in the world and say We knew you were Christians. We saw you, we knew you were Christians. We go home collapse into separate beds. Sizdeh Bedar. I am always asking about the massacre of Tabriz and the Marxist Muslims. You will notice most of them are waving it aside. Ah yes, the German says, I think the woman or something got some of what do you call it thrown in her face in the bazaar for baring her face for showing her face for having a face. You mustn't go there without your shroud. At Hatam the best meal in town is being served separately to women in chadors and children while the men sit 2 booths away. This is Tehran worse than Chile. But 2000 Marxists murdered in Tabriz where are they buried? Please note the beautiful stretch of land, Biblical, perhaps you find it here. Weep o weep children of the desert. Please note this wires me this wires me & no drinking in India. You are nothing please, however, that liquor may be purchased duty free at the borders and cigarettes from Kathmandu only $4 a box—$12 for us Indians, could you bring me some please Madam?

I have been walking in circles on Connaught Circle and before that and before that and before that and before that and before that I have been walking in circles and a long waiting period when I watched the women with their little ankle strap tall highheel pumps beneath shrouds. Black satin and patent leather and tough shaped painted eyebrows lifting in a Muslim world. And the little girls with dark blue scarves like peasants and they are so old already I was wondering it all in rials. "Khaheash-mi-Konam," I want to understand please. Pardon sorry, "Bebakshid." And before that and before that and before that Cable Blue Mosque to the young men recruited for the army and the eyes of the boy on the Bosphorus whose eyes are they? You said whose eyes are they? They are a woman's eyes. Deep pools of women eyes, black and huge I am sinking into. The young boys crowd around my young friend in his black Turkish beret. You are American? French? English? Leather? Cheap bus? Hasheesh? Change money?

"CABLE BLUE MOSQUE"

Paula's a real cockney. Note she's working at Naval Academy Tehran, for 12 thousand dollars a year expects to pack it in when she's got it together to buy a house in Holland or England. There are brawny Yugoslavs on Mihan buses seeking work. Everyone to work and making money making money. It is possible. Scent of blood. I've been out of the Muslim world 30 hours now and the shrouds are haunting me. I am going to get me one of them. Pizza Cowboys is probably not the best place to eat in Tehran but Paprika's got a nice name. Receive this wire please from not what I seem: American now wearing cowboy shirt, light green corduroy pants, gold belt and Chinese slippers. I stepped outside to observe the birds at sunset 2 days after Bedar day in a hotel cable "Manhood." The birds are whirling like Sufis so excited by the bloom in the magenta bush outside my window. Tehran is one of the higher cities in the world (at Mehrabad Airport 3,931 feet above sea level and northward at Darband suburb rises to almost 6,000 feet) but I have come down whew landed in India tropical sorta leaving the Muslim world. J193934 please to return to me I am nothing without my number pass. Ah, the German says, it is ok here. I do my work and though I can't read the numbers on the meters I can understand when they are saying it. I am in Interior Decorating. I'm handsome German man with silk cravat, wavy blond hair, but Tabriz. . . . (waves his hand). Paula: but everyone's scared shit you know they don't even know what's going on, the papers are so censored got a friend who's told what to write, you know how it is. Yeah official number was 300 massacred in Tabriz in February but it's more like 2000 (gives a laugh) . . .

Cable me rupees. Cable me instructions. Cable me Blue Mosque. Gate 4 Home Office says it takes 6 weeks for permit to Sikkim and Bhutan. The monkeys seem to be laughing. Fill out this form please and for 2 photos I go to T. Pall on Connaught and there are 6 photos now of a barefaced woman. I have black shoes. I have a black shawl getting on and off train Venice, Belgrade, Sofia, Istanbul.

We arrived at 10 am. I could see the city across the water under a pretty dusty gold haze, and the delicate minarets to Allah's heaven. Bernard Fountain was getting off first class section just as we stopped to change money in a little kiosk by the train. You are French? I asked. You have been here before? Yes, nine years ago. Where do you suggest we stay? O the area around the Blue Mosque, the pudding shops. Very good and cheap. Cheap food. We walked further to a little tourist information bureau.

Change money? Kabul? Cheap Taxi? Cheap Hotel? all around us, chorusing. Fountain is delicate with little mustache. My friend passport No. H 3035357 is not keeping his eye on striped bag from Kalimpong trip Giorno Brownstein 1973 and Fountain says But here, you must watch this. Very dangerous. You have something stealing. He says with heed to heed all men no women all around us. We go to Blue Mosque pudding shops to Gungor Hotel name meaning I never knew. Persian blue wall in room, 80 lire cheap and cheap and noisy and we are not hippies says my friend. We move next day to the Hotel Ediz 280 lire hot water for twenty minutes. We are up where we can see a bit of the Bosphorus and sky and gulls. We eat cheap pudding shop kebob and salad and beer and visit Blue Mosque but first we visit Blue Mosque. We kill Christians in my head.

Note the graceful cascade of domes and semi-domes and the six slender minarets. This is the mosque of Sultan Ahmet I. Note instead of tympanic arches to north and south there are 2 more semi-domes making a quatrefoil design. See the mihrab which indicates the kible and the mimber (it's quite tall! and observe the narrow steps!) where the iman sits. A muezzin drones at 6 o'clock. The mosque is flooded with light from its 260 windows. It is very blue. Note the iznik tiles, some of the finest with their designs of flowers. The fabulous Kosem, wife of Sultan Ahmet, is buried here. There are hints and mumurs from all quarters.

OK BLUE MOSQUE

So three days later (after Easter on the Bosphorus, not a glimpse of Easter in a Muslim world, we kill all Christians) we meet Bernard Fountain at the bus station down from the Blue Mosque. We're all waiting for the same bus from the shady men I was remembering the lewd men of the Muslim world and their past beauty eyes on me when the bus never comes. Some say she's a bit run down at the heels, but ah, Stamboul, what memories! We go eat stuffed mussels from the Bosphorus and Fountain says: "You know it's funny how I warned you to be so careful when I should have been the one. This guy comes right up to me right as I'm leaving the station and maybe I'm a little sleepy from the train all the way from Paris but right away he says you want to change money to rupees I know a really good deal with a friend of mine and since I know I'll want to stay in India a long time I'm thinking it's a good idea. He says how much and I am thinking 200 dollars I am traveling with dollars and he says you must do this: He picks up a paper bag off the street. You must put your money in a paper bag and then give it to the guy and he'll give you your bag with the rupees. He demonstrates by putting my money in the bag and slipping it into his pocket and then hands it right back to me. Now I'll go get my friend. I'll meet you in that pudding shop. I sat and waited and had a tea and he wasn't coming and I thought that's strange and I was thinking something was wrong. Then I opened the bag and there were pieces of torn paper inside. He was a fast one. Said he lived in a camper outside of town with his Austrian wife."

Note now Fountain is $200 less in Afghanistan. We said goodbye at the border when we were turned back by the scary uniformed men strutting around in their Muslim world, lifesize photos of the Shah as ruler of the universe. "Nix Barf" meaning no snow, said the Persian driver of the Mac truck and "Turkish, phew!" And after that and after that and after that and after that a Fundamentalist points to Mt. Ararat says, "There's a big ship up there."

And my lover, too, still with the men on the buses who were always coming to squat by my side with their lewd looks. And somewhere I saw a woman smile.

OK "CABLE BLUE MOSQUE"

Many lifetimes speaking and these are the elements of the 83-ship plan from the Western world for fiscal 1979 through 1983 (note: passport expires January 17, 1983):

New surface warships. One conventionally powered carrier to be funded in fiscal 1980; one nuclear cruiser funded in fiscal 1983; seven DDG-47 destroyers; 26 FFG-7 patrol frigates. Modernization of surface warships. Two Forrestal class carriers; 10 DDG-2 destroyers. Nuclear submarines. Six Trident Missile Boats and five SSN-688 attack submarines. Amphibious ships. One LSD-41 to be funded in fiscal 1981 and a second in fiscal 1983. The Marine Corps sought more. Ant submar and port ships Twelve Tagos ocean surveill hips one oiler; seagoing tugs one able repair one converted argo. . . . . Trails off here . . .

I have been out of the Muslim world out of the Western world out of the Christian world I have been out of the world 48 hours. Many lifetimes. I saw a woman smile. Then three pilots and Airport Control Tower Staff saw 20 Unidentified Flying Objects which were 20 times larger than a jumbo jet. Note: Pilots of domestic aircraft Mohammad Birami and Hassan Belaghi then reported seeing numbers of distant objects "flying over our heads." A second UFO report came from an Air France pilot at 40,000 which claimed that bright objects moving very fast between Shiraz and Isfahan were causing atmospheric disturbances. There are hints and murmurs from all quarters. And an unidentified flying pilot aboard his aircraft says he saw and exchanged signals with glittering bodies poised above him. When he switched on his front lights the UFO did the same using a strong type of ray which could have been an exchange or a warning. Also please remember to note that in September 1976 the pilots of two Imperial Iranian air force jet fighters contacted the Mehrabad control tower saying they saw an object half the size of the moon as seen from the earth, radiating violet, orange, and white light about three times as strong as moonlight. A man held his strong field glasses on his hotel balcony and saw a UFO emitting blue and red lights. Some say the thing chased them before rejoining the mother craft and flying away many many times the speed of sound.

       put in:
       commodities
       put in new-found seas
       put in courtesy & wit
       put in groveling wit
       put in symmetry
       put in coffin cords & a bell
       put in extreme breathing
       put in a cosmic image
       put in a feminine image

put in politics, brass-tacks level
put in how he was in love with Turkish eyes
put in is this machine recording
put in like footprints of a bird on the sky
put in lifting arms embargo
put in when you are cherished
put in still a little bit up in the air

"CABLE BLUE MOSQUE. CABLE INSTRUCTIONS. KEEP THE SHROUD OF THEIR PAST BEAUTY EYES ON ME. CABLE MANHOOD. CABLE RUPEES."

Note: Joachim X. German of Vancouver Canada traveling abroad a year as a self-proclaimed Evangelist said, pointing to Mt. Ararat its top shrouded in clouds, "You know, there's a big ship up there."

"CABLE INSTRUCTIONS DATA PAULA FOUNTAIN SHAH TWO CHRISTIAN ARMENIAN PERSIAN TRUCK DRIVER LOVER JOACHIM X. 'JIMMY' CHINESE MEDICINE HINDU PETE GERMAN (WAVES IT ASIDE)"

The ribs of Noah's ark are covered with black pitch and locked in the snow. I follow the Bible, J. said, that is my guide book. I will go down to the Caspian Sea.

Note: Nineteen year old Reza Bazargani took a stroll in the woods near Chalus on the 13th day, birthday Sizdeh Bedar and claims to have been "whisked away." "I saw the thing emerge from the sky and stop directly above me. I was unable to move as four space beings came out of the space ship and took me inside. The next thing I remember is I woke up back on earth in the morning, not in the lush Caspian forests but near Isfahan."

Dear Control: I am not what I seem. Cable my womanhood. Cable a black shroud emitting blue and red lights. The monkeys seem to be laughing. There are hints and murmurs from all quarters. I am not what I seem Ascendant Leo 4 degrees prose speaking leaving the Muslim leaving the Western world. I am not what I seem J193934 from capital city. But "CABLE BLUE MOSQUE," delicate minarets lifting to Allah's blue heaven.

I will go down to the Caspian Sea and weep for the slaughtered of Iran. When I return to the Harem quarters the black eunuchs will bathe me.

New Delhi
April 1978

Polemic

World's gone as usual askew
Don't ask. Ask
Take in the dark view

Iraq & rest of world hallucinate a public stew
A stuck market crashes
A small child falls in a well. It's true

World's gone askew
How you grew from once-young-lass
Then suddenly thrown into dark view

Darker view, Confusion too. It's blue
in the face, keeps going farther brash
Good monks, tortured, riot in Tibet anew

Just causes, hard facts everywhere for you
& everyone to crash about, flail
What to do? Take in the dark view

Who's got a clue?
What's the ration or station?
World's askew, bruised nations
Take in the dark view. Darker view
Ask. Don't. Ask

Managua Sketches

Christian Santos the poet led me into her home. An apartment set a ways off a main dirt road. The wind pushed through the jalousie slats, and she bent down to retrieve the piece of twisted metal that had gone clattering to the stone floor. "This is a fragment of the plane Hasenfus was shot down in." Christian Santos replaced the artifact gingerly, proudly, in a constellation of precariously set nails. "This is proof of the deception." I nodded. "The soldiers presented it to me as I was leaving the Front. They are like my sons." Christian Santos the Mother wept. "Perhaps you, Gringa, should go to the Truth. It is very—how do you say? . . . *Direct*. You can't even get sentimental, there is no time." She wept longer here. "Reality is not the problem. How do you say? Ah yes, it is the *Deception*." She pounced on that word again, spit it into the air. It bit and settled in the hot air. "Your CIA, I'm sorry. . . . Not *yours*, of course, I mean . . ." The wind gushed through again. The metal relic went flying. She smiled and shrugged. "You see, this war is terribly sad."

♦

(Reading appropriately here of Tezcatlipoca, Aztec "Smoking Mirror," which reflects, always, some version of destruction. The fragile sense always of that potential manifesting here. The issues are cloudy, and basically in these times and systems ones of materialism. The demon conqueror, hungry for territory. Put up a military base. What is the subtext to replace the cycle of Earth—Life—Corn—Man? "Nicaragua" is such a pretty word. Evidently William Casey could never say it. "Nicarga" he used to say.)

♦

"Better to live in your own country," Christian Santos the poet says as we sit drinking beer over the Laguna. She points to the ruins of Somoza's prison. "My grandfather Samuel was tortured in there. They'd butcher the bodies and throw them in the Lake. O precious blood!" Everyone I met had a story of life under The Butcher. "Better to live in your own country, survive as Witness if you can." Earlier in the day

87

her daughter's friend, the handsome seventeen-year-old, carriage and manners of a prince, was off to the Front. He wore his uniform courageously. He had come to say goodbye. Politely. Gallantly, to assuage our fear. No tears. How do you write a poem about this?

♦

We drive down Ho Chi Minh Avenue. "And what is the name of that flower? The intense red one?" I ask. "Pasquas. It blooms from December to February with great passion."

♦

Later we're looking for a tire for her car. The cars (many older Russian models) have a kind of faceless identity. It takes months to find a tire that fits. We drive to an old shack on the outskirts of town, and the young man working there is most sympathetic. "Come back in three weeks." There is always a dampening to any spontaneous optimism. There's been no coffee for sale for two days. Toilet paper has run out. A train badly in need of repair (parts) derailed recently, killing many passengers. "How long can this strangulation, the war, the embargoes go on?" I ask Christian Santos. "As long as it takes." Christian Santos is a fighter.

♦

Last night I dream my son (safe at home) has turned into a little Nicaraguan boy in tattered clothes. He plays all alone in a very spare playground. The jungle gym is a hologram. He is disturbed by its lack of substance.

♦

I hitch a ride in a truck with a cracked windshield owned by two brothers. "We are not happy under these Sandinistas. Life is too hard! But we want the freedom to be who we are. No big country to tell us what to be." They tease me about having only one child, at my age! They take me straight to the door.

♦

Christian Santos, mother of six children, works for the Sandinista Oficina Legal de la Mujer, a small agency with five women lawyers that advises women of their legal rights. There is much rejoicing as the new constitution has just been ratified, granting women equal status in matters of property and work. And the rights for the Miskito Indians is another area of pride. The revolution ripped through the fabric of so many lives. "Women liberated overnight," as someone puts it. Christian Santos would not go back to her husband as he wanted her to after the Revolution, be confined to the domestic stage. He is still angry and won't let the youngest son live with her. "Macho man," she laughs. The beautiful writer Gioconda had to abandon her son after her passionate love affair with a comrade at the Front. The gentle, quiet Vice Minister of Culture Vidaluz's husband is with the Contra. Broken hearts and sacrifice. Exigencies of war.

♦

At Los Ranchos restaurant I said something frivolous to the British actor Julian Fellowes about wearing a Sandino watch (he wore a Mickey Mouse watch), and the elderly Nicaraguan statesman gave me a long look. Not hard, but penetrating.

♦

Reading the clear poems of Leonel Rugama, died at age twenty in a shootout.

♦

The Australian ambassador is visibly nervous as I walk into the restaurant Los Ranchos with the Nica Rasta poet Carlos Rigby with his terrifying dreadlocks. "They, over there, have their own aborigine problem," Carlos whispers. I said to the ambassador how impressed I was that Nicaraguans had so "much heart, much poetry." "Yes," he quipped. "There's plenty of *that* to go around!"

♦

Christian Santos and I are getting dolled up for the reception at the little official Art Center. We've moved the precious lightbulb from the small room I've been sharing with the black rat who is quite decent really—his nocturnal activities so far confined to shuffling in an old box in the closet—into the bathroom. So we can get our makeup on. "You look so pale tonight, Anna." She has quite a patina going herself. "More lipstick?" We're both wearing high heels, which make a fierce clatter on the stone floor. Her friend Rico, the officer, has arrived from the Front. It's business as usual there, he implies. He has an old car we slip into.

The roads are quite dark. Dim functional lighting. We'd had no water for fourteen hours. Suddenly the car is smoking and sputtering. A bomb? No, a common malfunction, Rico assures us. Christian Santos is visibly disturbed. It really is seething now, and we frantically spill onto the sidewalk, running a distance as we expect it to fully explode. Rico rips some wires out of the hood. It dies, is sluggish spent beast now. A couple has stepped from their home onto the sidewalk, offering assistance. The man brings out a rocking chair from another century, insisting I sit down while the woman and Christian Santos discover they have friends in common. Rico goes off for help, for a flashlight, a tow truck, something. . . . We're having a friendly chat when he returns, profusely apologetic to me, putters around the car and pronounces the situation hopeless. "We'll just have to PUSH," he exclaims. The couple's little boy joins in. Street urchins magically appear out of the shadows to help. We are huffing and laughing. Christian Santos and I keep getting our heels caught in the road. About a mile. The children disappear as mysteriously as they'd arrived as we're greeted at the door by Roberto and Joe. "What happened to you? Ice is scarce. There's some rum and imitation Coca-Cola and a few crackers left." The paintings are colorful and fierce. Sharp angular lines, vibrating war-torn landscapes.

Glasnost

I would be her
I would be here and hear her be
I would be she
I would hear she, be she
together, her & she

& be stripped again, buttoned down. Would be drunk in the
movie when they put the father away, a Nazi. Write the discovery of
    being
a German girl. How torrid. How nasty. Put out her eyes? The war
I grew beyond, as any daughter knows.

And the other? And below, the masses keep scrambling.
Would be kept alive behind closed doors. Glasnost.
To reside inside a Russian word, give me the key.
Give me your jolt, your joy. Get down to it, woman.
I would be her slave in writing.
What do you know?

I know "glas"
I know "nost"

—obligatory?
—& the way she speaks
—you mean right inside the thing?
   the way she speaks inside the thing?
—thing meaning "you two." I meant meaning a couple.
   You know the meaning?
—I know it well
—but what confused me in the plot was the way the dog knew.
   Keeps coming back. In the middle of a war. The instinct
   animals have for their rulers
—but the two women, remember there were two of them . . .
—I remember, two of them . . .

—& they escaped
—& they escaped
—Ingrid had her eyes in heaven with the Lord
—& the German girl had a sweet tooth. They were filmic.
   They grew in the writing of them. They rehearsed a lot
—They were fit to be tied
—They got out in time

Russian Nelli

Come, Russian Nelli
who detests cold anarchy
That she busies herself within the house is good
O Come, Nelli, come
Discard chill treatments of stone & breath
Russian Nelli, Come

A valve in decorum speaks to you
Come, Nelli, come
a mere valve in a garden of wolves
who mask their ferocity
Come, Nelli, Come, they speak to you
Come, Nelli, Come Come

Which life of all is the best
in this old warring world
Do you like it hot or cold?
Come, Nelli, come
Before they challenge your wages
& ladle up the soup, Nelli, come

Find the *paroles* to enjoy the day
the diplomats all agree
that she who slaves will finish last
& sign a heavenly treaty
Nelli says she loves her home
"It winds me down" she sings
Nelli says she loves the globe

"It spins, it spins" she sings.

Andreas

I could tell right away he was German from his gruff Italian, the way he immediately dominated our little group at the Caffè Teatro. He was talking to Rosanna about Scriabin, what a fantastic composer he is, seems he'd just been playing him on the phonograph. He smoked his cigar in a big and imposing way. On hearing I was a poet and going to give a reading at the University he said he'd come and "have a laugh," but hoped I wasn't bringing over any more of that American decadence. "I hate John Cage," he boomed. When asked how I liked Germany I said I liked Hilka's bookstore in Hamburg—very bohemian—he said he hated things bohemian. But tapping my head affectionately he said he rather liked my dark red angora beret. Then he confided, "I am hard on myself as well and hate that which is not perfect."

Swiss Banker

Lunch on the train. Two bottles of wine. He is young. Handsome, vulnerable. The waiter is pleased to have placed us together and is taking credit for our lively conversation, humming to himself like an opera tenor as he waltzes down the aisle, a weighty man. Of course by now we are quite animated. I'll call the banker Johannes. He is to Salzburg, where his father-in-law is treating him to the celebrated Mozart festival. You can imagine he is greatly looking forward to this. Music is a pleasure he and his in-law share. His wife, he is newly married, stays home. He wears an elegant sweater. We talk about the Allies. About war in general. About the role of Japan. Why Japan hesitates. He explains to me about money. How complicated money is. I know this. Money is *always* the mystery. He champions the Allies. And then with all my heart in my own language I try to make him understand the pain of physical suffering. How many sorties by now, 55,000? How many Iraqis already maimed, murdered, how many innocents slaughtered, marines in panic, downed on sea and land? You would have to bleed in front of this man.

I would like to take his pretty head in my arms, cradle him like a baby, have him suck at my breasts and taste the milk that doesn't go down like oil, that doesn't go down like money, like molten gold. That leaves a sweet taste in the mouth. Does he forget? I am the innocent, I am always the innocent.

Sex & Intrigue
(She Seduces a Terrorist & Has
to Leave Town. . . .)

for Kathy Acker

She continues her memoirs, which seem more scurrilous and inventive from the outside. She escapes Rome disguised as a man. She has the gift of prophecy through dreaming. She has a photo memory. Example:

The decline in M.'s fortunes bring him to a frenzy. He starts to write a book denouncing D., and declares that A. was his mistress. The tzarina (A.) ignores his letter, refusing to buy the scandalous manuscript for an immense sum. Then it all goes to an American magazine but one considered *sotterraneo-pubblicazione*, or "underground." Thing is, Nameless sees the magazine 4 months before its appearance. In dreaming she sees the careless offset, the flimsy photo cover with its blue lettering announcing the title: BOLD. She warns A. but the tzarina doesn't care. This, of course, has repercussions with Z., J. and S. The tzarina seems immune to scandal. She's very young and inexperienced, doesn't know her own mind. "I shall take up dominoes in my spare time," she says. Soon she topples. This might sound like another century but it's not. Another example of Nameless's powers is:

There's been a so-called terrorist abduction. It's the well-known "pyramid structure," so C. doesn't know who are his (immediate) superiors. Nameless adores C., he reminds her of her own (lost) brother. He has been left "holding the bag." Another comrade has fallen. She, on the other hand, has tried to steer clear of politics but it is difficult when one has a lover. Surely you understand. He takes her very fiercely when he is angry. She doesn't think him capable of murder though he has been trained quite well. After the comrade falls, C. must almost immediately abandon his simple flat in Siena and his motorcycle. Too conspicuous. If only he knew who is his immediate supervisor in Germany, in Palestine.

They have just made love. Nameless is stroking the blond hair on his chest. He says: "If only it could be revealed." She sees perfectly clearly on his chest a holograph of the back of a man's head. A very thick neck with dark slicked-back hair. Slowly the head turns. Nameless describes the man's face to C. in detail (he has no gift for this vision). "Ah, why, it's Ruchetti, but he . . . I don't understand! He's Mafioso! Dio mio!" C. exclaims. Perhaps this young anarchist is turning to God? "We have been betrayed." He weeps now and Nameless consoles him, but she realizes too that her life is in jeopardy. They cannot stay together. Slowly and sadly she gathers her things and departs. She has a vision of a long train ride, first to Rome.

The next day *La Repubblica* deplores the gangland-style murder of Nunziatto. There is also a new communiqué from the terrorists which revives the old myth (see Gilgamesh tablets):

THE BRIGHT MOTHER OF THE HOLLOW FORMED EVERYTHING. THE PATRIARCHAL GODS ARE REVOLTING. SHE IS THE DOMINANT SEX, CONCEPTION IS BY THE WIND, THE EATING OF BEANS, OR THE ACCIDENTAL SWALLOWING OF AN INSECT. SHE IS THE WANDERING MOON. WE WILL DESTROY MARDUK, THE BABYLONIAN CITY GOD AND THESE OTHER FATHER GODS. THE QUEEN SHOULD NEVER HAVE GRANTED HIM EXECUTIVE POWER.

Nameless sees with her second sight that it will be a useless struggle but a bloody one. She wonders about C. and all the men and if this is simply another ploy to gain time. She wonders about betrayal. It might be a harder time for women, so she cuts her hair and leaves Rome. There are obviously some provocateurs at work. . . .

Okay the Dream

    loaded
& covered
        medieval wagons
or
armored vehicles
        swat team
none fatigued
"under house arrest"
beaten back
destruction of house & dams

our hut was dark

you saw the peace talk
you saw the delegation to Paris
you looked out the window of the airplane
you were once my lover

"revulsion abroad
& home"
was in my shoes
shoring up for the millennium

    now, a beach, a deserted stage
            child's
eyes gone

Amsterdam

Past Club Paradiso
Turkish rock 'n' roll tonight
30 guilden I'll pass
discreetly lit
Rijksmuseum—
majestic Rembrandts inside
I know they exist I saw them
The Anatomy Lesson of Dr. Joan Deyman,
Susanna & her Elders
Ecce Homo, Saskia
Titus at his desk
portraits aching to be touched
Guy from Bombay tries to pick me up
Just one drink—at your place?
Mistake I'd told him
just a chat he startled me
I'd been to India 4 times
Safe at Hotel now
Old Dutch hippie's herb gift at hand

BOM BOM SHIVAYA

Argument

Up the night with elegant former secretary
to Holland's Prime Minister
argue politics and Buddhism
He pitches back my false notes
goes for naive jugular
—is attraction at the edge of opposites?—
What do I know?
"The Gulf War was clean"
But I say
"Derek, how many loose cannons
do we need on the gundeck of state?"
7 a.m. His house resembles Vermeer interior
light steals in on the chessboard tiles
One more glass of wine—Prost!
Put all the demons to rest

2 A.M. Toulouse

Heady talk in La Garona restaurant after poetry show
Cathars argue separatism
The difference, Serge says, lies in the two gospels of St. John
The word "le" in front of "nothing":

1. the nothing nothing

2. "and without Him was *no thing* made that was made"

D'accord.

"Un Armagnac?"

Olympic Flame

The Olympic flame comes to Toulouse
in the snow

red on white

citizens throw snowballs
from the Pont Neuf into maroon-dark Garonne

Could be the Middle Ages
Tou Louse—Temple of Light

Slow taxi
skids
Worry will Jean next to me
get to the Gare to catch his plane
to Paris on time?

After the Greek

Tiny acropolises:
I dreamed
you were back
Oxen moved through you
It was the time of the junta
Poke those who do not jump for the ruling class
Die, Outspoken

ANACREON,

You are true
to the goddess
She won't shoot
you down
(Cranial Cronos is dead)
Yap plenty in her honor, now

TO NYSUS

Tough Opposition
from officialdom
to a sandaled god
Yet quick wits
always get you crowds
New women
hexed in your favor
O exit now
to the hills
Etiquette
demands ecstasy
in this cult

"Don't shuttle me around
padding dresses
Eros doesn't care
when I'm buck naked
I'll be outspoken—
You're all jackals or yokels
after the same tricks!"

Keeping Abreast in Bangkok

A gang of transvestites has been robbing tourists
after enticing them to suck their
tranquilizer-laced nipples, the police said today.

Four transvestites and a woman
were arrested in Bangkok after complaints
were received from a Syrian and a Hong Kong tourist.
The Syrian said he was robbed of a Rolex watch and $4,000 in cash.

The transvestites were smeared with tranquilizers,
as many of the tourists do not drink.
A standby tactic used by the gang was
to feed the tourists chocolates laced with tranquilizers.

Rat Temple

Linking the name and the thing not a simple operation
What we see walking Calcutta streets, not a vision
Night here, not just another night
People drop to sleep where you might be standing
Roll up under a structure of old tin
Sleep, sleep, blue gods & goddesses, sleep
Gutters are labyrinthian complexes of rat life
Not a passing mirage
We visit the rat temple to wish the rat a better life
That he come back a cow
That he come back Siva
That he clean up his act
That his sharp eyes be the wisdom of the scholar
That his teeth cut dualistic fixation
O blue gods, give the rat another lifetime elsewhere
Mother rat, you are energy misconstrued
I can't lift a stick to you
Become a naga, go live in Kohīma
Live with the Scythians in disguise
Monsoon, please come and wash the rat away!
Something makes its first movement away from itself
& utters OM, go away from yourself, rat, and sing this sound
Become something else, a beetle, a moth
When the lizard clucks, the women beat the floor & say
"Krishna, Krishna"

Must Be New Jersey

Later we're looking at the India slides
new-style temples, plaster with
garish color
ostentatious shiny red buxom Hanumans,
full-breasted devi girls, plump & pink
with ruby lips
"Heh," says the boy
"It's just like Trump's Taj Mahal in Atlantic City
They even got the rickshaws & dancing girls!"

Aside: A Jot

"The fighting has been raging since dawn" comes live coverage in Sarajevo. Raging since . . . ? The prick or sting of—something like ego? Fighting with myself, mid of night, what battle lurks there? I think what I was thinking back inside the covers was who maintains? or how maintain this bodyblood mind? (but not to slip into old defense pattern) for the true benefit of others. Becomes choiceless the work to do, it's "cut out" to do already. To write. And I think what makes poetry work is intrinsic built-in contradiction of absolute and relative truth. And people are dying. People are being slaughtered, are dying.

Oppositional Poetics

How do we now navigate a new chaos of possibility? Our languages and investigations of utopias, prehistoric caves, history's revision from a people's point of view, i.e. the invasion of Turtle Island ("these were the violent beginnings of an intricate system of technology, business, politics, and culture that would dominate the world for the next five centuries"). Pratitya Samutpada is a handy term to conjure here from Buddhist psychology which underscores the interconnectedness, the cause & effect—the endless karmic web of action. If you do this to that this happens or that to that to that to that to that this happens. How navigate the "horbins," or holocausts in memory, out of memory & to come? Is it conceivable? Dare we say oppositional is a *spiritual poetics*? How navigate mythological poetic wars, planetary finitude, unfathomable sickness, starvation & death. How navigate the new savage state? As writers what's the task? More letters to immured powermongers? New hope in a fresh, less cynical "administration"? Putting our energy onto quote a "candidate"? Total candor? Total renunciation? The Crips & Bloods the newspapers say orchestrate a kind of truce since the L.A. Insurrection, people to people we are made. My best friend & I argue about that word: insurrection. Want to get the facts straight. Is it simply a "frustration"? A looting? You think "riot" is a better nomer? Some of us think since Jan 17, 1991, everything's markedly different. My niece had "communist" smeared across her highschool locker for refusing to salute the flag during Desert Storm in upstate New York. No never sleep. You go against the grain for the benefit of others.

As the muse said to Hilda Doolittle, "Write, write or die."

Curse

This read dramatically with slow crescendo, building as it moves.

You loathsome miserable draconian TV patriarchs,
obsolete Senators,
questionable House of Reps,
lie-of-the-land Admirals,
perjuring Lieutenant Colonels,
dishrag attorney generals,
namby-pamby political pentecostals,
macho drug smugglers,
killer arms dealers,
consultant traffickers in blood money,
multimillion-dollar-fraud Pentagon schemers,
techno-military-industrial-complex corrupt Wedtech lowlifes,
Silverado mainliners,
slimy presidential wannabes

SHUT OFF

Not a woman amongst ya!

Ye lily-livered walloping big wheels

Judges of my world?

I'll make your semen dry up

YOUR GENITALIA WILL WITHER IN THE WIND

Insurrection

Night media told
urgent weight of
stories, that
there would
be grace too, and
violence, and
rage

and there was always

Rage of color.

and there was always

Come ah coming
down here to a
color America,
the best America

Remember
Frederick Douglass
& prophecy

who
you
are?

and there was always . . .

Surprised?

way off . . .

That a man be king
that he topple a dome,
L.A.
the syndrome.

But how many suffer
in the particulars?

You've got some stats?

numbers of underclass?

true? about the
number of blacks
in prison?

come on down to a riot
of color, America

get real

color (& there was always)
rage

young, able-
bodied

vast array of
shame on us

what planet
what community
travels

against,
its own.
Own what?

Own when?
how?

Tell the networks
to bow their heads
& place a garland here

for the dead
& Malcolm

for the dead O
&
Malcolm

Wrecked America
How to say what
happened

Place a tribute
for the dead
&
Martin

O for the dead
& Martin

a kind of
cause & effect
centuries waiting
the prophets were bold

"Who you
who you *be*?"

Abortion

The government does not own my body . . .

What hag might I invoke?

What madwoman who ate her own children
  gobbled them whole

What goddess of ache & sweat troubled & abandoned

What madonna who suckles babe strokes troubled head
  in wee hours he's feverish can't breathe body heaves
  she'll gladly exchange her life for his

I summon you hags out of chthonic caverns
  to witness madness here

To witness desiccation & lack of moisture here

Can you see woman held at gunpoint for the dark deed

Another in gaping poverty—see her? you see?

Already 3 swollen bellies to feed

Another with demon-eyes—see her, hags? See her?
  Father stole her maidenhead now she's big with child

There's one ancestor whose mate worked at the glass factory,
  forbade more children, will you cross him now?

Who looks down watering these bodies with tears?

Hungry in another country, how many girl children drowned?

114

How many born dead or die young nothing to eat

What hag can pacify pain of mother & babe untimely ripped from
womb

You think it's easy?

You think it's easy?

It's the breaking point, but it's my body

El gobierno no es dueño de mi cuerpo

El gobierno no es dueño de mi voz

El gobierno no es dueño de mi mente!

Abortion Rights Rally
Boulder, Colorado

115

Environmental Event

Record the bird song inside the oak wind
Lift the microphone to the tree
You must be outside for this
Outside, make a list of friends you gave to, you fought against, you
worshipped
Put their names in sacred packets, small pouches you prepared for the
names
Name the trees as you stand in the meadow
Shout the names of the trees
Spell the trees' names loudly at first then cast down to a whisper
You will be tangled in your hair from the wind
You will be wild
Take the packets and scatter them
Record the above, the wind and the packets being thrown as you shout
the locations of the friends—where they live now—beloved ones
who are animate and dancing
Later make a loop of the sounds (you are back inside now) and play
them to yourself
Visualize the notes of the bird
Visualize the oak, the names of lovers & friends emblazoned in the
wind inside their pouches
Visualize the coral beaches and ice-locked shores of the material world
Visualize the meadow you just stepped out of
The packets and their names again
Oak leaves in the wind
Name the other trees, aspen and poplar
The loop is a brown magnetic strip
Everyone, everything has a cycle, a circle
Hear through the window through the wind the sound phenomena
makes
Play back phenomena, you have a voice of steel

Michael & Amy in mind

116

Paean: May I Speak Thus?

Litany against AIDS

best read with a steady drumbeat

Lovers:
May you be inside each other,
traveling in each other's bodies like fire
May you be inside each other traveling like fire
Will you? Will you?
May the chemistry be good, inside a fire
May you be close in sweat & loving
Look at each other
brown brown black black white white yellow yellow red red
inside a fire
May the chemistry be good
May you be right for each other
May I speak these things? Of love like fire?
Burning together all conceptions
This is not destruction
This is the elements speaking together
    earth earth air air fire fire water water
    earth earth air air fire fire water water
& pray they be clean in you
& pray they be clean in us
& pray they be clean in you
Juices flowing, river rising
Juices flowing, river rising
Pray the chemistry be good
The water be good
You lie together on the earth
Breathe in the air
The breath of anyone who has ever lived
The breath of anything ever lived
Plants also, birds also
May the breath be transformed into fresh air

for anything that has ever lived
These are the elements speaking together
earth earth air air fire fire water water
earth earth air air fire fire water water
I say "Gather each other in your wind your fire
your air & pant like the good machine together"
Heave together
These are the rocks you thought could never be moved
These are mammals just coming out of water to air
Pant together, heave together
Travel inside each other like fire
May I speak thus of fire of body of river rising?
Knocking about in love
May the chemistry be good
Strum chords together in love
May your cells be suffused with light
May fire burn & cleanse what was a separation
Throw negativity in the fire!
Throw conceptions in the fire!
What happens next?
earth earth air air fire fire water water
earth earth air air fire fire water water
A new word speaking Will you? Will you?
May I? May I? May I speak thus?
Lift up, lift up, river rising
Moist earth sticks to your bodies
I speak these things of air air fire fire water water
earth earth air air
All elements speak together of this action
Bodies lunge in harmony, river rising
May it never be violent
May it be an agreement
May the elements be transforming
May your mind be present as you sup upon each other
May your mind be present as you drink each other in
Speech turns to the primal sounds of pleasure
The first vowels of pleasure

They wake the enemies of bed-making
Wake the enemies of love making
With "A" and "O" and "E" and "U" and "I-I-I-I"
   earth earth air air fire fire water water
   earth earth air air fire fire water water
The words aren't formed yet
But may I speak thus?
Speak of your fucking?
May I? May I?
May the liquids be clean in you
May there be no destruction
May the enemies be charmed at the gateway
May they work for you, may they work for us
May we dedicate this act to all those in sex sickness
& spread the merit in myriad directions
   earth earth air air fire fire water water
   earth earth air air fire fire water water

AIDS Benefit
Aspen, Colorado

Street Retreat

"Spare any change?"

We tried panhandling on Mulberry Street in the heart of Little Italy, a street with fancy Mafioso restaurants, espresso cafés, obligatory for tourists. People of all kinds, colors, some Europeans, Asian visitors passed us by repeatedly, embarrassed by our presence, annoyed, in some cases hostile. No one looked us in the eye. No one said, "Sorry, I can't help you out." I caught a wince now & then, slight recoiling. Were we junkies? AIDS victims? Pathetic? Anathema? Weird? Dangerous even? No engagement, no curiosity even. Cool chill up the spine. One of the former homeless we'd met said that was the most painful thing, it was just that: people don't look you in the eye, flinch as you hold out a hand. No human contact, that was the stab, forget money, you weren't accorded basic human contact. Invisible to them. Subhuman. An ancient broken man sat on the street down the block from us, rattling a few pathetic coins in a tin cup. . . . A centuries-old sound. . . . How long, Lord, how long?

We slept nearby on the cold pavement of Hester Street. 15 of us, 2 of us women having decided to stick together rather than brave the city shelters, where men & women were segregated, TB raged. We'd been told you need to sleep with your shoes on so they won't get stolen, and keep an eye open for sexual assault. Who could sleep?

Who could sleep on Hester Street? We gathered cardboard boxes from Chinatown, some with plastic peanut pellets, others with rice paper stuffing. Again we had the advice of savvy homeless, people who'd been out there years. Get the boxes in Chinatown. And we fashioned our cardboard condo. The street was cold. The cold seeped into your bones. What was that omnious sound passing by? Aggressive, merely drunk, indifferent? Was someone going to bash you on the head? Crush you in a box? Start a fight? Tell you to leave? Cops stopped to check on us their lights blinding. Garbage trucks raged like rutting elephants all night. . . . . . . up & down the street. . . . . up & down. You slept on a cold slab of a bed, you lay on psychological tenterhooks. You waited for dawn so you could walk to the Bowery Mission. Even sitting through 2 hours of a Born Again Bible-thumping service in order to get a little breakfast & weak tea in your belly was starting to look good. You visualized the food. You could wash your face & hands there, use the toilet. Rinse your mouth. You were feeling the call & rise of your animal nature. Survival. You were thinking of yourself, your urgent need to keep alive. Could anyone take that away from you? Night after night like this would you go mad?

April 1992
on retreat with Zen teacher Bernard
Glassman Sensei & other friends, N.Y.C.

Simulacrum (Not a Real Life, Cheap Imitation)

Coruscated distress
    condition or
contradiction makes
    strange of
brutal instances hiss & plague her

weird sister: genocide
    bruised, broken
locked in hallucination
    excoriate their crime
speak out & beyond

menace bodes ill
    ill shrieks ill
feeds on itself, seethes, writhes under
    literalization of death
loathing itself

bloated on greed, more greed
    to slaughter
whatever gets in your way
    land-grab, more slaughter
divide, nullify, murder, slaughter

& disempower a people
    erase a culture
how much abuse, dirty the river
    starve the mother, tighten the rope
consummate a dark plan

& glee all buried all done, dumped
    degraded, loathing, mass graves

bloody-handed Serb fired from a hilltop?
    there's history in it says the villain
& we are safe, excused, *the way we live now*

are we? (sever a neck)
    are we? (rather stand condemned)
never never topple (mock, deride the temple)
    political decorum
mistrust the infidel, heathen

sadistic life goes nourished
    psyche a shambles, grief
crawls in a dungeon
    twist inside victims' torment
incognito mask for slaughter

botched century votes
    another subhuman direction
eye lattice of wolf of garden
    of traffic, survived a dawn
pick up again, a dirty war, spit it out

what kind of life to live, spit it up
    when life is cheap
fucked over, codified, mechanistic
    armed, disarmed find a word:
armistice, now explain, dashed in semantics

only place is to live inside others' torment
    all response tinny
forlorn, knee-jerk liberal recoils in
    hounded night sound, horror
battered limb torn from limb

how won't any speak (scream or whimper)
    act, say stop, hold, enough
the unconscionable act

            headlines write in blood
Muslim child raped & dying in . . .

when they say a pool of blood
        a small thing, a very small thing
ruthlessly shot down, degraded body
            beyond recognition,
what takes to light your love just a child

silence from Mars, days dying
            silence from the sated
world, plagued
            of silence, damned to no speech
what takes to say your piece of silence swayed

the end of nature, we say
        glibly, dead of tongue of harangue
humanity in chains
        subjugated, bent to obfuscate
well-meaning crunch of any other tribe

death squadrons annihilate the senses
        what mouth-to-mouth resuscitates the ghost of night
what are we living for?
        what demon speaks in me to say
            I want us all to die

Cut-Up Amendment 2

*This written ("collaged") on occasion of public reading with novelist
   Ken Kesey at the Boulder Theatre, February 21, 1993, in Boulder,
   Colorado, after insufferable election passage of the discriminatory
   Amendment 2 in these spacious Rocky Mountains, whose passage
   will not go without serious question, injunction, battle, and now cer-
   tain defeat. This poem attempts to interfere with the brutal legalese
   of the Amendment, undermine its predatory nature. I used all its
   words, reassembled them, instilled a few images of my own, and in
   doing so subverted the amendment's power. As it is said in the Bud-
   dhist world: "May all beings enjoy profound, brilliant glory!"*

The proposed amendment to the Colorado Constitution
We will rise against won't fall by, rise by falling shapes lest defeat
   shapes us
Would prohibit the state, its branches
Of tree what is the alphabet? the inviolable integrity of language?
Or departments, or any of its agencies, political subdivisions
Self-renewing cycles of nature, language our own continuum
Municipalities and school districts from adopting or enforcing any
Negation of man or woman's past glee, but instead give rhythms of
   joyful speech
Diffusion of spirit, liberate the senses, don hats, shawls, wigs, scarves
Scratch any law or policy that entitles any person to claim discrim-
   ination
But disgust with a free country's mean law, not plausible
Crass, unromantic, give
Protected status, minority status, or quota preference
Based on gentle harmony not evaded & wrecked, otherwise cruel deeds
   abound
Against homosexual, lesbian, whose existences track the beginnings of
   civilization
Or bisexual sleep orientation, conduct, complex girl-bird epiphany
Homer to Daedalus, Sappho to now, vigorous song from way back
Practices, or relationships without mask, without fear, nothing obscene,

But ecstasy of purpose
And make all existing antidiscriminatory ordinances, laws, regulations
And policies heroic for all brothers & sisters too
Prohibiting discrimination based on individual's
Luminous mind, magnetism, sweet breath, eccentricity
Save homosexual endangered species, babble lesbian a world language
And bisexual ineffable wisdom orientation triumph
Unenforcable barbarity, claustrophobia & unconstitutional sexual
    grammar can't win!

Muse

I am this one writing to be more herself in the thought that all poems are invented by women. The night or nights of travel being a shaman of no particular society male or otherwise get spoken exactly like a love affair and are held as words. As words, these toward the beloved woman get mouthed, & she & I, or you & I or she & you come into being. It is my privilege to speak thus, it is my joy. The words are an event of no small passion and are forced from a place outside travel outside time. They arrive here too. And travel was the name & opportunity of the song as I was always a scribe & sidekick to her motion. She was my fixed star for a time of heart & I was perpetual motion too. I catch her as best I can/could through scent & ambiguity of verse. The pronouns you find us in in here are a relationship to secret notebooks and hallucinated masks. A relationship to a web of emptiness dotted with long molecules held near one another by the action of invisible forces. As forces were unified only for the smallest fraction of a second at the "beginning of time," so we both existed that way in words. The "shes" in it are our relationship. I am the mother most frequently & she too. And we are both daughters standing between the lines. And as children we both put on the shields like Amazons. O Sappho! I want to dance most of the time like a war dance. I feel the manifestation of speech like an ancient one. I always hear her coming back to me through many lifetimes, what a life to write of adoring her. Of adoring Her. Now is the chance.

The muse is always my opposite & opposing sister-singer. She is dark. I am simple. And light. She is not olive, but more a gray like coal beheld in a dream. She says that she is at the poem's service. To be loved & stripped & goaded & adored. Questioned, berated. She is somewhere to put verbs the poet bows down to taste these things of. Play & scorn. She is a semi-religious figure. Muse is brought everywhere to life when I chide her. That's the rub or night & day, the two of us. The chide that she not evanesce, that she never cease being difficult is the arising of the connection of power.

Written between edges of the scheme of particular parameters, the poems of her are of marrow made. The Muse is in marrow of me. The marrow made me a writer. So I write of her for that connection to first Mother-poem that carried in marrow. And was food & light & meat. I extend from here my first syllable "ma." It resides in the heart to be unlocked, to please the mother who talks inside me. All the manifestations of her: bitter sea. The taste of sea & sex & earth. As if you are in her cave. You've been there countless years. You live inside a circle of her words.

You came to Scandinavia to hold your own light. Trees live on every sidewalk. Mountain & sea & Fjord, & here was a land you recognized. Not a pseudonym underneath it. You were holding the light as it stayed at night. You could be illumined in your cave because you held the light of words. Sweet recognition of a point of tongue-origin barbed with love. She is a successful Muse & what legacy can only be approximated here. The Nordic goddesses descend in their teaching mode to instruct on the building of ships & shrines. Give us the wood again, they say.

Who reaps the joy of Muse in the sensual realm? She creates the motive to leap in words the love of our female bodies. Is she that hip? The line is drawn between words of dignity & those that do not further the gender cause. Light up. Light up. I am one of those of the *domos* of Sappho surely. And the cry of sister, sister, I know your sandals because I wear them too. Show me your parts. Who is she? The same age, the same build (a little smaller), size 8 or 10. She is the musk your dreams are made of. She is the terrible secret. She is enfant, Muse terrible. The lady that commands you acknowledge her above all else. And why don't I ever "get" it? To call her sister was always the call. I lighted on her plan to me as a confidant makes. She was not impressed. She conquers me.

The poems & how they'd form were always inside me, far back. I needed her as vehicle more than any father, rather to do battle. It's light out the window, 2 a.m. Goddesses walk the light sky. They tell me to keep the story up. They instruct a woman who was slumbering these long centuries to meet you.

Muse was a city. Muse was a road. Muse was my 20th century. For me she was a first civilization. She held me in primal arms, a child in patriarchal ruins. No she goes back further. Muse has arms like mine. Muse has my eyes, slightly aslant. Muse's wrists grow cold at night as

128

mine do. Muse sweeps her hair to one side. Muse colors her hair with the clay of Morocco. Muse's legs are pillars of exactitude & exertion. Muse holds her own torso of immense proportion. Muse was born under a sign of water & fire. Her sister Muse is the Bull-Headed-Woman. Muse crawled on her belly once. Muse never humbled herself before the guys. She stole fire back from the father. Muse took the fire and saw herself dancing in there, and the flames were the notes of my songs.

Pulse

She swallowed the drug with her whole heart.
She wanted to go that far, as far as she could stretch.
In her head she could be joined again in the imagination
of the demons who turned to archangels. She saw them
as flowers. She saw them as pliant dancing pulses
of energy, as light. She wanted to see the whole
scene again as it fractured into increments of life
and light, as it danced. It was a great dance.
She wanted to get on top of the hill where she could
look back at the town, where she could look toward
the sky. The sky was a screen for her mind to play
upon. She wanted to melt with the trees, with the
rocks, with the flesh of all the nameable world.
She loved words. She would name the world now.
She would name it again. Again. Name it words again.
She would embrace that hill and everything upon it.

She was coming down now. She had followed the deer to the
meadow. Her body ached. Her mind was still dancing.
It danced to her fear. She couldn't still herself.
She fell down. If only she could sink into that soil.
It was getting dark. Had she stayed too long? Had
she avoided staying with him, with one thing? Did they
need her anyway? Did anyone really love her as she
was meant to be loved, as she saw herself out on the hill?
As she saw herself as the lover who could love all of them,
any of them. Let them come to see me, she said. Her head ached.
She thought of all the ways to come down. She checked her
watch. She missed the others. Her red scarf was torn.
She checked her face in the car mirror. Her eye makeup was
smudged. She cleaned her face. She put on her
fuchsia lipstick. She could face the world.

Passion Being Writing

The way you describe any animal for slaughter
All its parts
thigh, breast, neckbone
savory in the kill with thought of blood-sustenance
I am that
or all those dimensions
The way varies of dimensions
Dimension of she
Empty womb today, tomorrow
How tally?
or shed
Breasts as food or supplication
as in beating them in a not-so-unhappy room
The written room
The already writing room
Waiting room
Forgive me, poets,
non-associative with gist of self and other
or mother-blind consciousness
dull in redundance when it goes ozonic
But take back baubles to adorn the sentences
& make her specific to inspection
I am indeed-the-now-instant
Ejaculating like the worst of them
And *puissance.*
You want my gold slippers, gold watch
You want my ring of fire
You want my gold handcuffs
good teeth
gold cunt, golden tits & ass
You want my golden eyes
that see ink as salvation
Ink of diamonds
Writing to wait the alchemist's death

To silence the ache of gold passion
Test me
The object is the conglomerate distances
'tween knee, ankle, rib cage, & jaw
hairline, stomach, the dimensions
38, 28, 38
8½ medium
4 inches,
3 centimeters (when cervix was dilating),
Size 10 throbbing.

Slaughter

Way you describe animal
"All its parts
thigh, breast, neckbone
savory in the kill with thought of blood-sustenance"
Way you describe
"I am that
or all those dimensions"
Way you describe varies the "dimensions"
Dimension of
Cervix, uterine mystery
How enter
or shed
Way it's put to
Breasts as food or supplication
as in beating them in a not-so-unhappy room
The written room
The already writing room
Waiting room
Forgive me, poets, the way you describe
"non-associative with gist of self and other
or mother-blind consciousness
dull in redundance when it goes ozonic"
Miltonic?
Way you describe
"But take back baubles to adorn the sentence
& make her 'it' specific to inspection"
Way you describe "indeed-the-now-instant"
Ejaculating like the worst of them
And *puissance & jouissance*
Way you describe how
You want gold slippers, gold watch
You want my ring of fire
You want those gold handcuffs
gold cunt, golden breast & ass or did you?

want them?
You want golden eyes
that see ink as salvation
Way you describe
"writing to wait the alchemist's death"
makes any woman shake

Rudeste

to the Muse, absent one night

She ne're visits. I want her perfecte
      & in manners tarrie for me

All women like her in prioryties of man & childe
      & then they would be myne

She lets it ryde her way & how in my supreme
      ego she not think on me nor ever send a sigh

I trouble her exceedinglie but I am void & numbe
      passions other ways lye, & sleepe

Then it's all over. I thought she loved my
      mynd, words, colors, habite

Swelled idea of cosmos, impatyence
      I loved her color, her mynd, her yearning

Her sicknesse, her obsession, her sliding
      & seeing all lyfe as writing, a genuine worldc.

Ms. Stein

Ms. Stein likes it with sunlight & a kitchen
Ms. Stein is proud of you, Alice
All the chairs are in an arrangement
Ms. Stein, Ms. Stein your nightlamp's on
Ms. Stein in a handsome suit with velvet trim
Head, you were a talking Buddha
She cuts down a recent visitor with a sentence
    about professionalism
I said she was a big woman: big belly,
    trunks for legs, feet on the ground
    sturdy pumps
She sits, legs apart, on a big chair
Is she walking with a cane
Holding her spine straight in Baltimore?
There was always talking & sitting
What was she thinking late at night
Was it this way to be working in Eternity
thinking: the present moment is the final reality?
She thinks: My ego's a sieve
I'm a big woman full of words

Two Men

Writing to one man of another. Now there are 2 &
I am writing of them. I write to one of them. I
write to one of them of the other one. Heart &
muscles and toes of men. Arms & legs & ears of men.
They are listening to hear about each other, one
to hear about the other one. I write of them.
I wrote to them. I write to one of them of the
other one. I write to him. I write to them.
They don't want to hear it. Writing of them.
Writing of them. They are next to one another
in my writing, now they are separated by my
writing. They might hate one another by my
writing. It could be romantic writing of them
to them. They look out different windows. They
hold me in common arms. I write to them. Is
it fair? Writing to one man of another one?
I write of them. I am writing of them & to them so
as you know me so they know me. I tell the truth
Eyes & mouths & fingers of men. 2 of them. I'm
not a wicked woman, I am writing of them. It
is harmless. Knees of men. It is harmless.
Thighs of men. It does not change anything.

H.D.

"split from Hesperus"

She said Join us
Challenges with a word
Catch verb-fervor

    "whirl"
            "splash"
    "hurl"
            "blunt"
    "trample"
            "spring"
      ("sway")

She is precisely armed
for the poem-chase

Lore

it was a mercy
her
bishop's thing
it swept shores
in decibels
classicism not
exempt for
her brutal
no—genteel—
arm
I have drunk too
much—you too?
she said
horns
a poesy's got me by
she said
not encroach
on this or any other
turf
but
love is
a country
go mercy for it
& capricious, a rasp
or
it was a
hinge hinted at
maps, boundaries
poets are saints in the sedge

in memoriam Elizabeth Bishop

The Problem

after Laura (Riding) Jackson

Shove feelings back
Then pull forward to tears
of years trying to get home-free

Soon, want home
Tears say *Go back*
I say I can't decide

Slowly, slowly, quicker, quick
Not tardily or I won't arrive
What does lover think?
Indecision. *She's late*

I'm late, see him
He's stern or cross

Old to fret
So touch him soft
I'm weak he's boss
I say *I'm not me till you get here*
So you decide, please

Live, how?

Heart unsure till it moves
Home city, no matter, proves.

Marianne Moore

And reading out from a manuscript
Her face, twilight beacon or alchemist's stone
Her offering was holy in us
For she offered light, and in the reading
A claim on us
Not negotiable
But held us in nimble wit
And danced from page to voice to ear
We listened and when she stopped
fell silent (fall, fall)
Eyed each other askance not wanting
To break it up
The "it" of spell, the "it" of
Impasse
She had those eyes
That went right through the next thing
Quickly
& music inexorably owned

Feminafesto

How different are times now for women writers, you ask. Woman any-
thing. Woman scientists! Woman Buddhists! My mother suffered her
creativity a scant generation ahead of me. She didn't have a "room of
her own." Her children were her work. Only in her sixties did she have
the confidence—with the support of a daughter & other women &
poet-publisher Leandro Katz—to publish her translations from the
French of César Moro and Greek of Anghelos Sikelianós. She died a
decade later playing the "spirit of heroin" in an off-Broadway produc-
tion of Burroughs's *Naked Lunch*. By then she was an embodiment for
me of the "hag" who had thrown off shackles of mean expectation,
could finally manifest beyond "girl," "wife," "mother." To some extent
she'd stopped measuring herself against a heterosexist world. She
would say to me, young, don't let men touch you until you "prove
yourself." What did that mean? Prove something to her? To "them"?
An onus I still carry. That a woman's sexuality and her work were
diametrically at odds? That you couldn't be "easy" & be respected for
anything else you might do? That the work was hieratic, untouchable
in some sense, but they, poor men, were confused and couldn't abide
a thinking woman. Or that I might be sidetracked, and have my true
passions of writing & "religious" study sidelined? That love would be
my downfall rather than Muse? And I wanted even then, young, to live
the fantasy of scholar-nun in comfortable albeit modest ivory tower,
away from secular and sexual temptations. The grinding care of hus-
band ("the quickest way to his heart is through his stomach") and chil-
dren. She said when I first married, "I swear if I see you pushing a
baby carriage a few months from now, I swear I'll come and shoot you."
She had a tall ambition for me and she was right to worry. For I was,
and still am, as they say—an incurable romantic. But little that has to
do with having a family. "A man needs a maid"? I never promised
domestic bliss.

And yet my father was a kind of heroic figure, survived the war,
returned home from Germany sobered by his experience, bringing
spoils—Nazi bayonets, medals, haunting images. He was sensitive, lit-
erate, former bohemian "piano player," a frustrated novelist. As

couple—both had been married previously and my mother with one son—they were optimistic about building on some kind of ashes, shards of war, Depression, Prohibition. Things must have looked brighter. And he went to school on the G.I. Bill—all the way through a doctorate at Columbia University. My mother had been a college Freshman-year dropout, wanting to study painting, went to Provincetown, a distinctly alternative artistic community, then married age 19 the son of the famous Greek poet Sikelianós and sailed off to Greece the next day for a decade. She was close to her mother-in-law, Eva Palmer, Maine stock, libertarian, who donned the garments she herself wove in classical Greek style and kept her red hair long. Eva had been close to Natalie Barney in Paris and was part of that exotic cluster of lesbian and bisexual artists and poets who were dissatisfied with expectations back home and lived in a self-imposed ritualized exile. Gertrude Stein was another. My mother met Isadora Duncan in Greece. After a little more than a decade that chapter of her life was "closed." Divorce, the war, back to Provincetown, matured, met my father at an Isamu Noguchi party. He was living next door to John Dos Passos. They fell in love. A second marriage. Not that he held her back exactly. It was a condition to be in of the times. And you merge with the man in an imitation of enlightenment. Joining the "other," joining the "light." How close can you get?

All my teachers in the formative years were male. I especially remember Mr. Grief at P.S. 8, our poetry teacher, who would hold female students by the scruff of their necks and bend them out the window. "Mr. Grief brings us Grief" was the common chant, like "Rose is a rose is a rose." He was clearly disdainful of the "girls"; they were lesser beings. High-school teacher Jon Beck Shank was gay, a blessing, whose recitations of classic and modern poetry I will never forget, nor his sympathy with quote "the girls." Because we were soft on poetry too? My male teachers in college thought us dilettantes. Always that persistent need to prove oneself. Get serious. Cut class. Write a poem. One of my mentors, Howard Nemerov, said to me,"You are both a peasant and a queen." What did that mean? More categories of definition in a heterosexist world. And when I went to meet my first Buddhist teacher, Mongolian lama Geshe Wangyal, age 18, my boyfriend pleaded take off your lipstick, please, it's disrespectful! And a husband could say with accusation, You are just like all the male poets. Just like Robert Creeley! Traveling the globe leaving hearth & home, abandoning child, jawing with other poets till the wee hours, god knows, how can I trust you? And how could he? For I wanted this other path, *desperately*. Poet, outrider, free woman. I could hold my own with the boys, I could "drink like a man"! I could "talk like a man"! Of course I'd always identified with the male protagonists in the novels I voraciously read as a kid. I was the constant reader. And I was hungry for their adventure. I wanted to be right inside Balzac's *monde*, hang out with actresses & dandies, twist in fatal political & love intrigues. I would follow, I would "live" Siddhārtha's journey through the words of Herman Hesse. I had a box of exotic costumes. Favored disguise: Robin Hood, Prince Charming, Annie Oakley, priest. I played a character called Tomboy Jo, and Shakespeare's "merry wanderer of the night" Puck in grade school before I grew tender breasts. A later age I would yearn to play first Hamlet, then King Lear. And I saw myself as Puer, picaresque adventurer, traveler in boy garb, entering the Hindu temple in Puri strictly forbidden to women, or making the long Haj, the pilgrimage to Mecca. Do you have to be circumscribed? Do you really have to be circumcised? Women are considered "sebel," unclean, in Bali. You are forbidden to enter temples if you are menstruating. You wear the *chador*, which covers all but your eyes but even those must be lowered, averted in narrow Arab streets. Your power, your nakedness would cause men to go mad, commit unspeakable deeds. Would change the world! Would paint it scarlet. Would seize & restore the night, an old control. Check out the Levite laws in the Bible, the destruction of the Ashtoreth goddess temples. Your passion would run amok, make riot. Your multiple orgasms, your oceans of bliss, your "cum" would flood the world!

When I came into power as a writer, and I think this had to do with becoming a mother as well, I could say outrageous things, could proclaim my "endometrium shedding." Could manifest the "crack in the world." I shouted, "You men who came out of my belly, out of my world, BACK OFF!" I could literally stomp & "walk on the periphery of the world." I could—as Sumerian Inanna did—get the male poets (my fathers) intoxicated on alcohol, Methedrine, ecstasy, charm them with my wit, my piety, then seal their secrets. I could name all the various women who have been, to be. Cast a discerning eye at the progressive anthologies of poetry. Are we still having to count the men versus women, and the canon is a lost cause or perhaps it is the battleground? Look at the scarcity of women in any institution, sacred or secular. Keep counting. How many pinks to so many blues? Is language phallogocentric? Is writing a political act? Do you women writers I'm speaking to feel marginalized? Do you agree, you'd almost have to, dear scholarly sisters, that the experiences of women in and with literature are different from those of men? Much feminist criticism has centered on the misogyny of literary practice—women as angels or monsters, mothers or nuns, daughters or whores—harassment of women in classic & popular male literature and text. You know it: Kerouac, Mailer, Henry Miller, Homer, the Bible, the Koran, the Vinaya, et cetera. But I'd like here to declare an enlightened poetics, an androgynous poetics, a poetics defined by your primal energy not by a heterosexist world that must measure every word, act against itself. Not by a norm that assumes a dominant note subordinating, mistreating, excluding any other possibility. In fact, you could be a man with a "lesbian" consciousness in you, a woman with a "gay" consciousness inside. I propose a utopian creative field where we are defined by our *energy*, not by gender. I propose a transsexual literature, a hemaphroditic literature, a transvestite literature, and finally a poetics of transformation beyond gender. That just sings its wisdom. That the body be an extension of energy, that we are not defined by our sexual positions as men or women in bed or on the page. That the page not be empty female awaiting penetration by dark phallic ink-juice. That masculine and feminine energies be perhaps comprehended in the Buddhist sense of *Prajna* and *Upāya*, wisdom and skillful means, which exist in *all* sentient beings. That these energies co-exist and are essential one to the other. That poetry is perceived as a kind of *siddhi* or magical accomplishment that understands these fundamental energies.

Perhaps women have the advantage of producing a radically disruptive and subversive kind of writing right now because they are experiencing the current imbalances and contradictions that drive them to it. They are turning to skillful means figuring how to combat assaults on their intelligence and time. She—the practitioner—wishes to explore and dance with everything in the culture which is unsung,

145

mute, and controversial so that she may subvert the existing systems that repress and misunderstand feminine "difference." She'll take on the subjects of censorship and abortion and sexual harassment. She'll challenge her fathers, her husband, male companions, spiritual teachers. Turn the language body upside down. What does it look like?

Writing

And putting my hand to my body examine a body. And putting it thus to a body examine a body. I stroke the top of my head from the part down. The hair is asymmetrical. It stops short on one side like a boy's, and on the other it bobs out. I put my hand to a body examine a body. And putting it thus to a body examine a body. Underneath, near the neck the hairs are dyed black, they're wiry. I caress my neck, skin soft under the chin. I pull at my earlobes, chilled to give them back life. I place both hands over my face as if to apply water, apply cream. I bite my fingers to feel alive. Then my face feels my fingers, my hands, slightly rough. And putting a hand to a body examine a body. I touch my lids, what eyes look back through my touch?

I can't stand to feel this desire at attention, at desk.
I lie down. I touch myself between the legs. You imagine
the rest.

I return. It is the same. Ah, the desire, ah the writing,
the fulfilling of the writing.
At desk, the writing
Ah the writing
At bed, the desire
At desk, the desire Ah the desire,
Ah but the writing.

Desire, Ah writing
& putting my hand to a body examine a body
I never get out of writing but getting out to desire,
It was an arrival from desk to bed & back
Ah the desire
Ah the writing

I touch my breasts, yes I touched them. Imagine the rest.

To the Censorious Ones

(Jesse Helms & others . . .)

This chant accompanied by a chorus of women flexing their muscles.
First performed at the Naropa Institute.

I'm coming up out of the tomb, Men of War
Just when you thought you had me down, in place, hidden
I'm coming up now
Can you feel the ground rumble under your feet?
It's breaking apart, it's turning over, it's pushing up
It's thrusting into your point of view, your private property
O Men of War, Censorious Ones!
GET READY BIG BOYS GET READY
I'm coming up now
I'm coming up with all that was hidden
Get ready, Big Boys, get ready
I'm coming up with all you wanted buried,
All the hermetic texts with stories in them of hot & dangerous women
Women with lascivious tongues, sharp eyes & claws
I've been working out, my muscles are strong
I'm pushing up the earth with all you try to censor
All the iconoclasm & bravado you scorn
All the taunts against your banner & salute
I'm coming up from Hell with all you ever suppressed
All the dark fantasies, all the dregs are coming back
I'm leading them back up now
They're going to bark & scoff & rage & bite
I'm opening the box
BOO!

Talisman

unraveling scarf, a jeweled scarf owned since childhood

    also a protection cord, a strangling cord, a shelter

    a blanket

    a tent

    a coat of many colors

I concentrate on this cloth:
it's a burial shroud
it's stolen, it's a skirt
it's a hiding place, it's not easy
it's bloody
it's for a marriage
it's been worn before
violent tapestry, it covers the face
      I carry it I wear it for you
      I put it on you, I place it on the table
      It takes up space, I can rape you if you're wearing it
      I can smother you, we can make love under it
      It's a tablecloth
      It's made by the hands of Indian slave women
      So I give it to you & wear it for you
      to please you with its ambience & death vibe.

Crime Work
After the Holocaust

At the breakfast banquet all there is to eat there is to eat is cigarette butts. It's after the holocaust but everybody's got their glitter. I'm wearing the doubloon won't buy anything in this century perversely from the person I hate the most & I'm wearing the shiny belt I think I'll strangle someone with but is it possible? & you've got your scorpion pin with the red glass eyes & rhinestones you bought to cheer yourself when you hated me & we've got knives & forks but nothing to eat. German coins. Nothing to eat. It's after the holocaust. Everyone's wearing jewels & scarves & pins & St. Christopher medals & William Burroughs medals & we're decked out but there's nothing to eat. Can't eat metal can't eat stone. So there will be starvation for all unless there's a crime to end all hunger end all opulence. Let's get it over with I'm hungry. No one to buy our objects. No money. No food. I'll be the assassin. I'll take responsibility it'll be me. If I kill we can eat & it'll be cannibalism but we'll survive another week. I think I hate you it's got to be you. I pray to myself to forgive myself. I call on all female deities wrathful & compassionate. I call on all death guardians. I weep for my mother's flesh. Her legs. Then there's a compromise. I throw the sticks whose number are all of us present. The black one is the Chief. The red ones are the women & there are others. So who will it be? How to eliminate. Chance & fairness & we'd go hungry if we were stronger & we could go hungry we could go hungry if we were stronger. I need food. I am food. I am food. I need food. I am the last stick I am very Oriental. I do myself in & it goes like this: You tricked me. You flattered me. You touched me:

> They laid me out on the table all decked out,
> scratched me with their metal & I bled &
> they began sucking & eating. And you were the
> last to partake & that was when I didn't care
> anymore, love or hate. And you were going to
> love me when we abolished hunger.

My Lady

I wish to speak to you about my lady
Very clear streams speaking among themselves
Since there is so much bliss in these words
"Ladies refined & sensitive in love"
I tuck these words away in memory
You who pass by the way of love hold your gaze too long
And the desire to write & the fear of beginning
The canzone has power to whoever hearing listens
Then I compose the mention of my lady
As I walk out, the pelt of hunted game
Some of these things are always looking at me
My words tied in one with the great mountains
The white musician turns black
It's the Black Chieftain dream again
Grown up with the neighborhood & how it squeezes me
Bone-tied, bone-dry, ossicles, the caribou
She & this number are synonymous

O my lady! It is I who dream too late
In these words that praise my lady
To everyone who captured listens
The keen & lofty minds all night dream of you
And Jupiter in sky, frozen silent pods the poets passed thru
And inwardly explode in persona del'anima dolente
The little heart replies to her "Your face proclaims
Subtle tales & pieces of crystal"
My lady my lady is obvious

my lady my lady is obvious
my lady my lady bleeds
someday we will talk of this
my lady my lady
my lady drives me mad she's so finicky
my lady my lady

dolorosa rosas & pine, my lady my lady
she wants the crown, my lady my silly lady
my lady just sits & stares, my lady my lady
my lady tells a story in the night
my lady sweeps the floor
my lady goes out to tell the truth
my lady frowns, she scorns

my lady has a memory, my lady my lady
my lady has NO memory, my lady my lady
she never forgets me she feels the sleeping spirit in her breast
my lady my lady
my lady rides the Appaloosa
my lady protects the environment
my lady's heart belongs to daddy
this much, my lady, I understand

I love my lady she drives me mad
I love her tragedies
& the way she undoes me
my lady my lady

How I Became Biblical

The boundary of my might wanting to be agreed upon. I travel like a note, or rather I perform as a note, a communication, a tone of definite pitch. I pitch in, sometimes out of range, a high "A," ebullient, like some wild bird cry. I listen to myself and become Biblical. Then I sit down on this wide earth (Africa, Asia, South America) never to suffer again but to take on all the colors of effort it takes to be born this way. And borne along by my traveling companions, the winds, and borne along by the seed of men too, and carried the world over. I wish it for the sake of variety, complexity, science. Now see my intertidal being in all its glow and the hoopla surrounding it. I take my passport into the street to be my home metaphorically, the street which in this terroristic age could be the place of display of all freedoms & demons granted since the very beginning. I create it in my mind, too, add to it knowledge of trees, of birds, of circuitry, of static, of coded messages, Molotov cocktails. My belly would be a target and my face a reflection of phenomena's desire. I would be the necessary vowels & consonants too, and condescend to speak with the breath of my 5 ancient sisters: the Winds of Thrusting, Hiding, Summoning, Gentle & Wheel. I meet them in the deserts of the world. I summon them up when you aren't looking. My scope & map are dedicated to sound reason. And my view through this lens is my passion. Let it disturb the porous, and crack the solid. It is this way I travel out of sound to be one of milk & sorrow, and one of strength & metal.

Yum Yab

How many heads,
wily, cynical do I have?
How many snakes hiss forth this skull
How many arms to clasp the lover
who trembles, shudders
in multiple embrace
How many adornments,
weapons, power implements, planets
are wielded thus, thrust about,
spinning their whizz and gleam
How much spittle, menses,
blood, lymph,
tears, urine
does it take to turn it around
How many pores on how many breasts
arms & legs
Exits, entrances to carry you through
How many mouths
to speak your name = Deity Masculine =
& you return in another form, purified
lopped off, never emasculated
but diminished of arrogance
liberated from an old karmic push
Master of the Universe
released to become subservient
before we become equals
& you will play the other side, try it
you will be objectified in my lists & games
Together we ride
Together we ride
& you will be my gratified desire
Enter the gate—
gate of cervix
How you are finally my doll

my puppet, lost brother
my split-off side
processed, shaped by largesse, by rage
by bondage
How many times I ask for retribution,
ask you be placed here
astride my body
as consort, as adornment
as lateral mind
as thinking into absolutes
not a chance encounter
no histories of the men loom here
Erase the obvious ones
who seek dominion
who plundered the womb
who would only conquer what they fear
Turn it around
Retrace the steps
Back, back
uncover the ancestor
Recalcitrant one
Who bore you first?
This rocks the plan, this is the
first spark
latitudinous
unrehearsed
a broken form
Picture a monument
a state of mind
a lowing beast, a head held high
a last resort, a lay public
a hieratic thrust, a witness to
exploits monetary, & sexual
a scowl, a forehead that
looks as if thinking
that blazes its many fiery tongues
a tonsure, hope's envy

to be fortified by night
to be exquisitely decked out by day
naked, absolute, over a fine edge,
sleep ridden, driven by dream
Power is not her metaphor
yet estranged from her shore
languishing for cities
lusting for completion
divided against herself
and needing you, ornament,
my subjugated "other."

The Sofa Is Black

Monsieur is here. I am reading. Reading the novel. In it a woman feigns ill is reclining on a sofa is revived but wants to die in the arms of her lover. Lover is monsieur is here. Am here reading. She says in the 18th century she wants to be caressed by the arms of death and the phallus of death. She is feigning. He, another Frenchman, the architect, wants none if it and I want none of it he says. He is monsieur the husband. He, another one who loved her once got tired. Got tired reclined on a sofa. The war continues beneath their balconies. *Voile* is not the order of the day but volley might be. They (the countries) play war beneath their shuttered windows. He picks up the pen to write to his mistress "They play as if at war beneath my shuttered windows. . . ."

She remembers the first day her mother said Save your leg hair for shaving later you want something to look forward to. And she, another one, a nun, dropped out, became a mistress. Of any household, dust & sweep, dust & sweep. She is like to strangle herself in mirror in the tedium of dust and sweep. But is rescued by any man who is Back Door Man who is the butler in any century Mommy (he heard it on A.M. radio), what is a gigolo?

She is another victim that week. He writes "I worry for you."

(We scan down the street to see brief lives.)

She was a mighty matchgirl and displayed her wares in the heyday watering spots all about town. She is secretly dealing a controlled substance. I love you I love you she cries to the cop who plugs her.

& Marietta Martine is the Mata Hari who stole in a bigger time at a bigger angle and developed her lethal weaponry to be marketed in Iran, secretly in Israel. I am reading. Monsieur is here. He gets up to gather his opium paraphernalia. What is a novel? In a title? In the act of? Of what? Someone is doing something. Someone is torturing someone.

157

Woman is being the victim of this or any other story. She is feigning to get the best of the plot. She is feigning until the denouement to show true colors. The sofa is green. No the sofa is red. No the sofa is blue. The sofa is blue. No the sofa is black. The sofa is black.

Under My Breath

Of memory there was also a song
of poems where people were bargaining
Forget these lootings that seem to sob
Forget there would be a way out
Where I am I say I repeat I am solidly about
not to go under
I need this one chance I need this to begin
This was one's friends, ungovernable like lifespan
thorny, tyrannical
They are all disloyal tonight!
This was one's friends, a lifespan
This was one's friends, to freely exhale,
Quick apprehension, see the game now
This was one's friends, you're duped
This was one's friends, a soft spot
This was one's friends, a tone, a loud consequence,
stiff, delicate, fierce, so odd a case over so-called "religion"
This was one's friends, no adequate forecast
This was it, this was one's friends, a calling
This was one's friends, I told you so
This was one's friends, 18 years ago,
you met his boat at the dock
This was one's friends, a wedding, kindness & ease,
operative charm
This was it, it was like this: friends in one's heart
It was like this—friends through a mist of other things
Traveled far since that evening,
since an afternoon in April
This was called waiting for one's friends
This was one's friends, supposing everything,
fatigue not in my line, believing all you hear,
a perceptible change in one of them,
wanting an excuse for not getting along with, or
susceptible, a big part was talking talking,

This was one's friends in a booth by the window
This was one's friends rarely a sad story
A friend jumped off a building and died
This was one's friends, we were out a lot
This was one's friends living in a city
One had friends in a town near the mountains
Impute to negligence, alterations, Time?
This was the way it was with one's friends
borrowing money from one's friends
eating dinner with one's friends
stopped in, an excursion to friends, working hard,
unmistakably one's friends
dazzling for one's friends, youth, powerplay,
a little sphere of misguided concern, control,
stammer, learn something about me
This was not significant but this was one's friends
My friends can't be bought
This was one's friends, the world became more interesting,
Extemporaneous, I see them repeatedly: my friends
My friends this is how they were: busy, funny, obscure
Behavior is a mystery to me, O friends
This was one's friends in an airplane
This was one's friends—formidable, reassuring,
suffering, peculiar
All the friends writing in luminosity: ogres & angels
How intensely I see them, how shiny they are!
What was the intent: they were shy & wonderful
or greatly in command of language
for amusement, for amusement was part of the song
of my friends, see them in the great desert of the years
Friends melted away
No, stay stay
How far can you go
But an enemy keeps close, an enemy full of vivacity
Enemy just darkened my path
One might imagine it—emptied shade.

Riddle a Geographic Ambition

Deities
of the
volcano
odd rock or cone formations
the battles
ascribed to Pele & her rivals
were fierce,
jut & spew
She always won

History
like any fiery
torch gives
her banishment
then
Migration
she's expelled
her distant homeland &
travels, travels
digging
testing the
earth to settle down
finally
digs a pit deep enough
to house a whole family in
cool comfort or
exhibit them in
spirit forms:
flame & cloud

Hawaii's creator *Moku-a-weoweo*
(Land of Burning)
is sanctuary,
end of life

for many
who border those
rims
she, a crater,
glow glows

In the little museum
inside a raging storm
the boy & I study
her wrath,
flows the
dioramic
narrative:

1. establishment of Pele's home
2. sending for her lover Lohiau to share this home
3. sister Hi'iaka betrays her, she's furious

Pele very beautiful with back straight as cliff,
breasts rounded like the moon

We walk to her edge

What is a human geography?
asks Ambrose
Imagine her,
I say,
earth-moving claws
her many tongues of flame
before she cools down

Early

for son Ambrose

so what? . . .
boy, are you Greek
without the Wisecrack god
       —LORINE NIEDECKER

family
truce
   a truss
of truth

die?
how?
and matter
how moves it
before a
mother's urn

she
of all
questions
quizzes the boy

are you
sweet baby?
& rings a song
for his ear
early

can't remember
he says
her or anyone then

but
some graph
or photo

near
table
swept
clear
of
tear

A daughter
gave birth?

a glass
on a mantel-
piece
reaches

it had roses in it
sobs
& gobs
of roses

Comes-with-a-Child

for radiant Althea

Problematic conjunctions with each other & with other things—
    beings who cluster in your life—shimmering, shifting,
        palpable, demanding, complex tone you take the lover on

Take on self-enclosure of romance, spin out to
    feed the child, take on his/her good omen
        "keeps you young," acres of sweet new speech

Patterned to forget your habit & grief
    for she who comes along is new child company
        bodes well the robust parallel, the song

Stuff to breeze by, to whittle your fancy, dictums
    friendly, stern, the boundary & discipline charms
        the household and what you can say about

A father, a mated man, the new ones' postwar boom conviction
    rapt, attentive, visibly placed, reads the stories well
        cleans up after the spill, swell of bloom & mess

Whispers edge of anecdote, folklore, cosmology
    that won't be elbowed aside by easy commerce's offers
        lists in heritage, pleasure, swarm of accounts

Receivable, its old connection: tribe & dream
    noble qualities of snow, landslide, ditch
        avalanches of word sinew, grammar of instance

Place a temperament to carry her pout & pouch
    her visible burden, a wild stab at parity, at
        liberty with a tender tone, still a baby head

And she with him, reserves the right to not be
    politic, polite even, tears his heart asunder
        goads his lassitude if ever could be called such

In him on to weave a fabric, illusory to all but
    her little heart, a net or cradle, old womb tales
        and he out of respect for all that woman conceives

Is really caught, blessings on a famous honesty
    rarely errant but a kind of bucking bronco head
        about him, arrows aimed at all he holds aloft

Held like a sack, a snake, a complete plant item,
    boxed and stem up, tray for excess, no parry on the floor
        no explicit wager or bet to afford a stance

A stance which in itself elicits epistemological zeal
    or does it? especially when objects come in
        unannounced, no warning but clumsy noise & tread

Not that they have lives the way we do, but the way
    a child might animate the doll, the spool,
        create a throne of discarded cardboard, precious

To be used, take a scissor to the plan, the way everything
    pointed must be an angel, and then you create a castle
        or jail—what shall it be?—and know your place

Among the knaves & knives, the sleeping princesses,
    the sails of hardy ships & voyages not yet mapped
        occasions for courage, foolish bravado, treasure hunts

Come under the table, put a blanket to the ground,
    set out all of creation for a viewing, ascribe it attributes, silence
        the enemies without, boys & dogs, and make a version of

Complete specialized risk, planet's quaint kinship
  layers of other beings—stuffed fox & elephant, old bear
    that will not speak, totem sanctuary for a crossing over

Not gender you say but scrawled handwriting, not clarified
  but left open to chance, immediate frivolity, tricks or
    games in which you hide, not alone but preceded

By satiric, comic overtones for the thrill of
  discovering the code, cracking it finally in your
    own hand, because young as you were you were never

In memory that young however blunt the truth you were
  says itself as you ponder his separate daughter, and
    earn a turbulent entry in between the two of them

Praise the sensibility what other constant images to be
  writ down: bird-girl, web fused with wood, all approval
    imagination gives, seminal or definitive behavior

As in talking of an eloquence, a grace of hand or twirl
  as one does singing all the while "I am the angel poet"
    and he—dazzling electrons the two of them?—by her side.

Kill or Cure

One can still fill whole books with descriptions
of enemies, prosperity has its dangers
In the virgin forest the sweet-toothed bear
stripped many a colony of honey stores
The digger wasp penetrated, then man followed suit
testing & smelling, taking what wasn't his
Standing beside his brother, a strong memory for place
and a larger & more demanding ear, eager for the music

Kill in the midst of the forests of night
expounding orthodox or singular (secular) aspects
of an imagination, any human, any common reader
rushing again for the daily newspaper which
facilitates, you think—perhaps mistakenly—
a discussion of relevant problems, a study of
the grand design, a stand on all the issues
acknowledging the dagger, the gun, the stick

A kind of metaphysical rebelliousness, wagering
positives, I know I do it too, loving more
wisely than ever before with an awestruck voice
a clever voice, a downside voice, on to the next topic
Rhetoric can't be easily explained in politics
The thing inside the thing, the object of this discourse
is precept rather than object, I take these vows
in meditation, that the truth never be a problem

Is the forest in error? Is the sun too?
Do we have our eyes in hell with the tyger?
Ambitious pride is ruling there with the Lords
of Materialism, the genius needs to aspire
beyond herself on wings of convoluted irony
The trouble is history, the trouble is primates,

faulty logic, late-night temper, polemical half-truths,
radiance of fame. Is power good or bad, simply?

I am a questioned-developing-thought
A gap in me, a gap in eternity, casual glances
caused by radiation, sketchy enthusiasm
by this thought struck dumb in the presence
of how do you say "emptiness"? which is filled
with light & energy, food for all of you
I want a thorough attention span, outrageous logic,
a sinew of wrath to kill, to cure

One may fill whole books the way she exits
the plane, the way the artificial light
is blinding the way the same Lords of Materialism
pierce her eye, & anything you want you can
get anywhere you are on this protracted
protected soil, in fact you needn't exert yourself
too far in any direction, others have been
hired to walk for you, to talk for you

To do your thinking on the Op Ed page
which is infuriating today in its
dumb one-man-upmanship point of view &
as I perceive it, lies, what to do about
it in a relative space for outside the sky darkens
the wind is intense but doesn't blow your cares
away, including that passion that rises up in you
towards all of them, the students, the protégés

Distract me from killing again the fool
in the castle, the youth's necessary
voyage I want to speed up towards some
kind of transmission, aw cut it out
Awe is the number as the plane wobbles
in my head now, and she or he or you too,
as the case may be, disembarks again,
& again faces the shopping malls of Florida

And again rushes to telephone home
like the stranded alien. The wires cross
in the complexity of the gulf stream too,
getting across the message, make contact
not simply to destroy but simply say "I exist"
But if I don't I do too in awareness
Take this body away on the next flight,
shake it down or just let it breathe

Hiding behind a cocktail and a polite quip
about economic viabilites in terms of
energy proposals for underdeveloped nations
This is a serious business, this is a serious
retaliation from the money world
& finger pointing & fist shaking
You'll come running when the time comes
I wish it would come soon like any good apocalypse

Turn the version upside down, roast it
over the coals then see what it looks like
It looks strange, it looks daunting, outmoded
& she (the image) resembles a dream of myself,
brittle charcoal dakini, so passionate she burned up
in fiery charnel ground doing more battle in the world
Yet light shines in spite of all you manufacture
It shines harder as it occurs to itself to go out

And this is the 5th sun according to the Maya
give it another chance, or round of applause
We kill each other as we speak to keep dominion
and kill as we love, shy by the fountain, angry
on the Spanish Steps, outraged in Bhopal
You name the place I'll be there, killing with my
thoughts, loving too—it's out on the street again—
stepping off the plane from Managua to Miami.

Go-Between Between

Language does more than merely communicate and "express." It arrives, it manifests, it is a relationship. We are all languages. Are language and culture really opposed, are speech and writing opposed, and what is the "dialogue" between *langue* and *parole*? What does this mean/matter to the poet? Does a text truly exist outside the world? How is "speech" inside the world? Do these questions come out of my western tradition—a tradition narrow in scope and finally irritating? Might I write such a large work that could exist like the Bible, the dictionary where the speech and the speech of myself to others could sound. I am personally interested in how my own writing and the writing of others *sound* in the world, how the writing initiates itself as sound first, how it resonates in my body, how it seems to move from heart to *hara* to mouth, how I perceive this reading others' texts on the page silently, and how the poets I pay attention to mouth "it." I am interested in how I personally manifest the psychological states that the "writing" activates and provokes, how I sound the different "voices" that I seize from, access, respond to, take out of books. How the writing is a kind of go-between between states of mind hidden and states of mind realized/enacted, as well as what's overheard. I wish always to pursue this relationship and push the experience beyond the page. Yet honoring, too, the page. That the page is a catchall. Page which is shapely, literate, and which originates as a kind of cosmic void. What hope and fear exist facing the blank white page? Does the computer change this stark joy? I am afraid of getting lost inside the machine, another kind of fear. I get up and dance when I can't sit still. I mouth the syllables. I play with the words. I play on the cosmic battlefield of the blank page and of the room's silence, for writing is a kind of war. And yet I take the words where I can get them and play out all the contradictions. I enjoy a large text to play inside of that could be like a dictionary or phone book.

In the Thai tradition, to interpret a text in a reading or performance is to "ti bot"—*to strike the text*, much the way you would sound or strike a musical gong. In my travels to Asia (particularly to various parts of India, Nepal, and Bali) and in my own ongoing study and practice of Tibetan Buddhism, I've noticed that the sound of the words has an intrinsic power. The word exists to both vibrate "out of" and also to enter the psycho-physical system as well as the larger environment (it's all interconnected). Seed syllables travel and carry certain efficacies. I heard two Vedic masters chanting for hours from the *Rig Veda* at a festival in Bhopal several years ago. They had been trained in this classical tradition since childhood. They were essentially priests of the texts, holders of the texts, and vessels for the wisdom and power of the texts. Yet each of them had a distinct—you could say almost a "personal"—style, and they were both *living* the Veda. Thus the audience was receiving a direct "hit" or transmission of the text through both the refinement of tradition as well as the immediate call to have it come alive/be actualized in performance. This performance contrasted with the appearance of the Bauls of Bengal, singers as well as dancers, during the same festival. The three Baul singers were performing work within a less refined yet more spontaneous street-tradition. The music has secular and sensual appeal. It's demonstrative, vibrant. They were dressed colorfully, with an androgynous aspect to their garb and gesture, in marked contrast to the pristine white-robed Vedic masters. And yet at root, both performances shared the premise of hitting the text, striking the form to achieve a kind of holy synchronized ecstasy. Both traditions exhibit highly evolved and subtle manifestations of "siddhi" (sacred energy or knowledge). I started also in Bali looking into time cycles.

The literature known as old Javanese (ninth century A.D., Java) has many poems written in the tradition of Sanskrit literature drawing on both Sanskrit and Javanese vocabularies. Each poem begins with a *manggala*, or invocation, that establishes the poet's understanding between him/her self, the text, and the world. The word *manggala* literally means "auspicious." A text called the "Sumanasantaka" begins by invoking the god of beauty (*Lango*), who is concealed in the dust of the pencil sharpened by the poet. Lango is asked to descend into the letters of the poem as if they were his temple. The god is not an external deity or saviour in the theistic sense, but rather a refined consciousness or sensibility—not "of" the relative world of the senses. Through this deity, one breaks through dualistic illusion to meet reality, as it is, face to face, without veils. Lango literally means "enraptured."

Lango joins man and nature together. So the deity is a kind of vehicle for realization of *things as they are*. This is a principle in the practices of Tibetan Buddhism as well. One invokes the yidams, or deities, as manifestations of more awakened states of mind (energy without ego is the idea here), invites them to descend, and unites with them. Similarly, traditional haiku works with a heaven-earth-man principle. Man, the concrete image in the haiku, is what joins heaven and earth. Lango is similar to the Sanskrit *rasa*. (Sanskrit poetry/poetics has its origins in the Vedic hymns circa 1,500 B.C.E.) *Rasa* literally meant liquid, sap, semen, but later became "the essence of a thing." According to Sanskrit poetics, the poet traditionally needed to possess "Vyutpatti," vast knowledge of the world (culture); "Abyhasa," a skill with language developed from constant practice and apprenticeship with a master; and "Sakti," creative power. Sakti relates to the sounding of the text. Mantra, in the Buddhist sense, is explained as that which protects the cohesiveness of the "Vajra mind." "Vajra" is the quality of clarity, indestructibility. The Vajra mind is diamond-like, "beyond arising and ceasing." Mantra is a means of transforming energy through sound, expressed by speech, breathing, and movement. Mantras are Sanskrit words of syllables and express the quintessence of the various energies with or without conceptual meaning. The Buddhist practitioner recognizes all sound as mantra, or from this poet's "absolute" point of view, all sound as poetry.

In travels to Bali I was aware again and again of the intrinsic power of words and how they are included as necessary parts of ritual activity, especially in the long *wayang kulit* (shadow puppet) performances. I was intrigued by how the *dalang* (priest-puppeteer) *moves* the languages around (he combines Kawi, high and low Balinese, and Bahasa Indonesia, the *lingua franca* of Indonesia, in one performance). All the realms, actual and psychological, are being invoked. He or she mouths many different voices that are literal texts of *The Ramayana* and *The Mahabharata* as well as spontaneous improvised comic banter. Although the epics exist as text, the *wayang* transmission is essentially an oral one. When we studied gamelan, we had no score or text. The teaching was purely on a visceral level. The *wayang* is a meticulously prescribed enactment, still the most popular form of ritual entertainment in Bali. It resonates with all ages and experience and may be heard on many levels: dream, history, battleground, personality, religion, pure sound and vision (the shadows are mere "illusions" on the screen). The idea of "ti bot" is highly evolved in this kind of performance. Language as such is more than a predictable medium of communication here, more than a mere system of signs, for it plays an ongoing role in the process of imagining and interpreting the world.

There's a patterning in my own nervous system that I enjoy and respect and manifest in my own writing and in the performance of my writing—it resonates with other patterns in the world. The describer, the artist, is always a person. We need these present eyeballs and ears and bodies to register "our world" as it flies. Every syllable is conscious, on and off the page. I am not interested in distancing the "audience" (myself) from the text, from the enactment of text. Thought and language are metabolically linked, and this psycho-physical system is also open to any pulses that arise. These typing fingers are transmitters. All the texts are throbbing with sound. I vocalize them to you. I type them to you.

Abróchese el Cinturón
de Seguridad

A modern erosion of what it had, was not lasting, a
speaking seamy side residing in lust & money under sun.
That was & that wasn't what only was. That was. Was
what? Miami. Miami corrupted the holiday. Lone
weathered arm, slow walk, edge of the elderly, their
edge on us. Sigh of the elderly sea in your ear:
invite your body here. Breathe audibly through
pouted lips. Play with the fringes, forget personal
violence. Torpor, while it has the appearance of
atmosphere, resides in the sand.

And was a police? Naked for want of a badge discipline.
It likes us browning to a crisp. Lie in the dirt, O
sun worshippers! Abróchese el Cinturón de Seguridad.
Invite the sea to your ear. Where is a tip of corruption?
On the tongue of police. Was and wasn't. A clever woman
is just a clever woman getting by & light to her eye
for a necessary sunshade. Sunscreen. Smoke screen.
Help them over the border, the workers of the world.
Social kaleidoscopes will marvel the escape.

Miami you could drown here. They hold you like knives.
Steady does it. For every woman I see I see the subtext
of weaponry, & don't take it out on me. She is saying
this as blind, as friends she can trust. Do I know this
from the street from the muse. I do. Do I know it from
myself. I know it from myself. Life. Tight. Rose.
Aquamarine. Late. Noise. Death. Alarm. Hispanic.
Message. Sign for. Soft. Close. Checklist. Medical.
Cocaine. Shave. Calibrate. Sea. Yours. He will come
tomorrow. Let me attend my bed. Intercourse first. Honduran.

What would sell? Mouth admiration, loneliness met
suddenly in an unlikely thought. Black shapeless mass
of water. "I believe all you women are crazy"
saith the police. Desultory warfare like a TV show.

Miami & you get the idea. Miami & you shed a little
nun's black clothing. Take off your shoes in Miami.
Like Borneo could be developing. Like some mysterious
work meant to work if you are an island. None of the
aliens are fond of one another saith the newspaper.
Competing in a dread of restraint, destiny in the
rough hands of any old sea-dog dealer. Diverting
attention from any possible levity. Plumage of birds.

Do I mention the palm trees? I do. Expression of her
(my) face now seen by rapid change.
One word of comfort like poker face. See mine too. Fresh
minted coins, claw-like fingers, low bow, full red lips.
Police will kill O these wretched I treasure. The stockade
in great demand & into the unknown Borneo. Rustle of trees.
I shook off the life & then I shook off the life.

More appalling than love is sex? Lady of the night cries
her eyes out near The Garden of Eden on 6th Street. Foolish
white men, put your penises back in the sheath. In dire
extremity she lives, lack of jest, & adds herself to the
picture twitching the corner.

Run.

Unless perhaps to take a snapshot. Lieutenant, say
something. Say the Law. Law something. The Law,
she murmurs piously. The law is like unto me a testicle,
a testifying man, a testament of someone's faith I had it
too, long ago. The Bay where police why not
money about a dirty business
teed off. Why not favors to get "it" (yourself) by.

El Salvador how to say it in Yiddish. Nicaragua how to
say it (yourself) neutral-like. What is now ancient off
the coast. Digging up the praxis of a dream. Help me!
help me! It's not all crooked here residing in sun.
Don't die here. It's not all wicked here. I see you
little girl landing to an escape hatch. I see the sun
metamorphosed as eye & yolk. Breakfast & freedom for all.
I see my frailty as I sink into dirt. The mind metamorphosed
as Latino beat. O momma!

Miami you took me in your benefits against nerve gas, a
cameo performance, a dark lit stage, the swell of the
crowd, a hoot and a holler, nostalgia for protest. Shame
the status quo. Miami you are quotable & high on the list
to never go into the return of the churchgoers. A showy
argument against playback. News may be untrue. There
are more lie days when I was young, yet all my words are true.

Here of manner. Apologetic smiles, secret shipments,
strung out on Marseilles Street. Once or twice a
prostitute. Flit across the street & settled here. Lips
move in the corner of the bodyguard. Where I slumber
distant chase, the TV show, heeded by three men playing
for life or death, goes on.

Goes on of savage things on beach, misgivings, an urge to
paddle, the backwater in question, hid the goods, no motive
of prudence could save us, standing certain of the police
& they were there.

I am much more than a vast extreme, she says. Eyes that
in every glance cite my lack of license & I do have a
license officer really I do. Folks floors above at the
Forte Towers name themselves for the pulsing strength
to exist at all high in the night. Freezing hallways.
A dip in the pool outback. Lime as a color, and crystal
as a chandelier, vying for supremacy. Why so tough, Madam?

Too many drugs & a cure? The beeper lures the worker to
another abuse. Spoke of better days, the investigator,
a white woman.

Down on Marseilles Street she files the report. You can't
release a baby to a condemned building. In another language,
you can't release a baby to a condemned building. You
need to test negative before you can test positively how
to straighten a bed. Ease up. You can't release the whole
night to your desire to be an addict, Madam.
All the juices in the tropics won't help your pain.

First Person

for Bernadette Mayer

A: I broke with the conventional world to get a little sleep.

B: This story is portable in intricate rug pattern, bookmatches, glassine envelopes, a laywoman's Bible.

A: Yellow Pages speed me where I go to manufacture & fix this heart, or techniques for future decoding, you name it. The telephone could always ring.

B: Why me?

A: Good at naming. Around a naming drone, the hours rotate. You're always in love, dulcimer-like. Or so you say & hope. Hope is everything before dinner.

B: Passionate hope. Read a few books about it. Preferably Science.

A: Hear it?

B: Is it mine or yours?

A: I have a black one, the non-interrupting kind.

B: Everything is still a wheel for a long time ago. I oversee my village with the outlook of a builder, inventor, sad pragmatist or half-back in a photocopy shop. Rain falls before I pick up my children.

A: Children love a rainfall. Maybe it's the pentatonic sound of memory of jewels from the Bronze Age.

B: I broke with the conventional world to study these things out: conventionally upset in St. Petersburg or wearing African chains to bridge shyness.

A: Tightening lug nuts in the 20th century!

B: Something . . .

A: As a once-big-leggy-time-attraction, I was separated from myself right before Mardi Gras, because Mother Russia built freeways & freight trains.

B: You don't mean past lives, I hope.

A: Future librarians & lab technicians will back me up.

B: Go howl in a fellaheen night.

A: Two fellows in an antique parking lot waved at me once. I wanted to tell them all about father-icon fabrications, urban fossils, our past.

B: Could anyone guess by this we're both women?

A: It's still mother's milk to the masses.

B: Patterns to protect us from ourselves.

A: Patterns from ourselves to protect.

Can't Touch This

Don't interrupt
  the flow face to face
    is you behaving oddly
      saw you there in the already daylight
        kiss never offered, syringe unused . . .
          & seized it back

Saw you as trouble on top of inspiration
  which had an even darker purpose
    & you tell me more about it
      how to build on manhood gone away
        less fascinated how a
          new coloration liquid flows in the body

A woman slowly revolves
  A sharp bell rings
    Little scrapes on the floor stand in for children
      Half-shut eyes look through a door
        as if a rajah loaded with diamonds were still possible
        & sound a warning, trepidation's juncture

Hot? Cold? Whose frame arches towards the others?
  makes tentative shuffles their direction
    approaches with a shining eye
      & monsyllabic commentary
        all the time trying to converse with passion
        "come towards me now"

Languid-appearing, an impulse to the contrary
  But this is someone who likes to dance
    Check her out in a careful study of peculiarities
      you'll see she loves the boy. She does.
        He's got "brains" to be proud of
          Likewise a priestess adores him too

Parsimonious with praise
    Elect to never say anything not of a thrift nature
        While the woman (me?) is hypnotic, inflicts herself on the crowd
            Predilection for trance
                River becomes ocean
                    Weds her to outside world

Respect is all pervasive & a slow accretion advertises
    Knowledge who appears in various body shapes
        invites no notions to the room
            Let them ring true with such intention
                Otherwise reiterate the pledge:
                    To innocence & more income!

That quaint map on wall is solid
    Not taking new borders to account
        Old theme: travel
            Before you get restless
                A clandestine can't-touch-this-kind-of-knot
                    Not starving for all the "sights"

Give way relating personal history so often
    Avoid certain places to love
        Bend your long leanness over me
            Improbable ruination of an hour
                Conscience thrives over a blessed body
                    You discover how taciturn

Keep open retreat
    Desire spins chorus of yes, o yes
        Fugitive dreams of vengeance too
            & fragments wait to be enslaved
                Now silver, now ebony
                    Difficult phases of the moon

What could be more wrung or wrong?
   Disdain, anger, murmur of revenge, a long sob
      Composure of quack variety pulls itself together
         the whole man, the complete woman, the half-man, half-woman
            half arrive & day goes firm, a graceful curve
               obedient to all their desire

Close to him-her, don't interfere, something runic written down
   What is it? Wait for disclosure
      Won't be undone for words
         Disturb the so-called wilderness
            to find what any heart will tell you
               In the face of you again, pouty

Approach a magisterial tree
   Its big eyes are alive again
      They are tree-eyes with an abrupt return to the past
         Ancient subjections, you name them
            Re-appearing over an uneasy world
               Reappear. You may grow up now

See the standing-around-aspect
   One can't argue with
      Yet what concerns the writer is
         The barrel of a weapon that fires many times
            But only shoots once
               Fear in the eye behind the sightline

Fear abuses the shadow then lets it evaporate
   Light scans position as you do
      Scan the features closely
         Outstretched arms, kneeling posture
            Don't kill this one in purposeless conflagration
               Victims, victims, no resistance now

Yet someone will cry, someone will be shot
   never come back to roost in that tree
      Catch up, all loops waiting to be broken
         Like the inner voice continues to be warlike
            After shadows of the outer courtyard fade
               Blood is no accident

Warm days, somber sky, no accident
   One sweep of the hand signifies immense sadness
      Get back, the world is bigger now with its keen breeze
         enigmatical relationships: how to understand it & you
            How to struggle toward sundown (I cry I lament)
               Accomplishment spoken of in an ordinary tongue

Rival paradigms are put to the test
   an evolutionary one
      & the other one people get lost in
         Is ignorance only provisional?
            Elucidate an old text?
               Will your sense of time circulate?

People vacillate in contradiction to themselves
   Absolve the devil who contradicts me as well
      & change his or her mind toward a darker light
         I try to be there with you & then I must be gone
            New errand beckons or haste required
               to defy a mission canceling desire

Is possible? Take the heat off please
   An edict passes from hand to hand, blinds further what's obscure
      But sings how to concede likeness
         Being so sure of you my opposite,
            How unalike, whether flippant—or under the current
               of some vast wing alone command the rest—we are.

Mauve Flowers of the Ubiquitous Wisteria

This lapse attributed to the most jarring
of opium
"Hello, monkey" they are saying for
"Hello, money"
I have misheard you, children
very sorry to be awake now to
undeviating aromatic shrub
in your lush places
You, children, dwelling high among
the clouds and rainbows and clear blue skies
while I (harsh blue-red wine)
Very sorry to be awake, tottering
under granite sky weeping
I think the secret dies with you, the monstrous
things without fur and feather
forfeit the art of leisure
The jade horse at grass beyond the ha-ha
skips and frolics while I
take a solitary dinner, an early dark bed

Code: Intensification of Shade

In the terrain
    & as time measured valuable
      —the farthest reaches of human time—
    The town grew to possess itself

Time became the pioneer
        on the move so that other species responded
boyhood on the move, matriarchy on the go
or sly

    To chill his sister back to land
omnivorous life so arranged as to be
    continguous to
        town
            Town as diverted trade, as endless settlement

& all it bodes
    & that, too, on the move, like time
Then time became
    a random aggregation of strangers

        Then town became
consanguinuity, more blood, faith,
    speech
      a well-knit priestly caste

Town became
    a prize for the fattest hog
for the austerity of
    some old other part

which was in no relation to
    shade, rest, economy

No relation to "sod corn"

> The gardens now going
> the Mason jar a thing of the past

Who wept?

  & stopped going restless for the wagon
    & rose above the emergency of weather
emergency of kith & kin

> Who wept?

a bond is still a bond
  rural delivery, telephones, an elder traffic,
    cyclonic storms

Time was never again numerous or attractive

Tract

The far corners of the New World are jumbled but real museums
of the remote antiquity of man.

—CARL SAUER

I live with them:
                          palms, scrubs, oaks
shrubs (I said) bunchgrass quickly maturing herbs
     (said quickly before an earth dissolves)
I live with them: many older forms
     with habits of eye, taste
  habit of
scent would be something to live with always
I lived with them : non hysodent horses
     Lived with passion
          wanting to photograph everything
(can't do that here said quickly to dissolve but mysterious
 Anasazi won't allow, said again can't strike can't shoot
because so beautiful . . .
     said this in a dream)

will burn later, so beautiful, will burn
vacant stores, burned out in insurrection

     a lady gone mad for hock & debt
Lived with a longer legal trial, America
Live in quiet about it said another tone: *riot*

          Live with sloths, mastodonts, giant camels
lived in fear in suffering
giant beaver, muskrat, cottontail

Bed down with bison, elk, musk-ox
    slept in an automobile once also
        was loved was eaten

ground squirrels, saber-toothed tiger,
he held me once I swear a tiger may be grand & gentle
      peccaries?
           those too
Browsing rather than grazing . . .
I lived but did I see
         I lived with the idea-edge of ghost-animals
           & ghost of swamp & arroyo
(someone tell quickly before story dissolves)

when someone (we) come to tramp & tread
when humans (we) come to dine
herbivores first O listen children hungry mouths
carnivores with blood-lust listen children
        O hungrier gut
& chew back life (why they did what they had done why did they?)
to spit out stolen gifts of pelt & prey
        I lived beyond extinction so far, you too children listen

—a terrible news

Replenish Making
Twine If You Like

for Andrew, to ascend those high places

1.

somehow dreamed together
        dish
it replenish
making twine
    if you like

tightly wolverine
he dropped
        ground

    breaking

there was wringing of hands

    because
any credible heart could

    beat how
work spoke
            come back to work
how work speaks

& shall swim
    tiniest flagellum
        to light

        so blew out his night
        like early light

enters a tent
     dawn light

& she blew her dream
   out like
       night speaks in harangues
she portrays in canvas
the life
       inside a bold actress

driving in a car, the . . .
 avoiding a house, the . . .
   avoid part she was playing

& her falling is
   in identity to new love

unfolding was
       magic
cacti in the yard

another person there
who is smart in poetry

     perched to drive
or drugs be driven

wolves singing
   within the man who speaks
a yipping

andros

he she loved

     his clipped heart

they were wandering
   wildly uncombed

avoid what?

   then tore at it
with pointed teeth

      stood before him
        a house in a forest
stood before him like a house

that dissolves into smaller house

severed to bits
      a nation's long war with itself
     &
      her head came apart
this was civil

       cortex explodes like a house,
a home

coda:

what matters is
we still had a bed
fashioned of twigs

who can sleep?

2.

                things seeking an exit?
or
excitement

"d'amore ancora"

our cooling
              —never

yet wheels the word
  clinging clanging to you

  (power tool in the clearing seen under
dew it was morning)

   divorce has power

& body is not driven dumb

but writes, speaks
in
  no woman's dished folly
    behind the wheel

   terrestrial means passion
in a house

  give us time
wheels of it

  time I give
  all the twine I give

3.

ask for you: poetry's mouth

ask for you
                    that
        beauty plies a trade in language

  ask for you not
    ask more but asking

  be what you rage about
        remain your way
etc. in the rough etc.

I mean to say a way away mean to say
        to power comes you

not yet
    mental phenomena, but
shocks
            search our demons
      out
      with fire they are too modern

burn! burn!

I pause to cut
in or out of
an old oak room

but
  stay on me demons
      burn

just not set sail

           appear
vowel after vowel
   or twist on
  tongue
to speed me on
    tiny wheels

handle it?
    a pump? a rein?

another person was there
smart in philosophy
who held a cord

sifted out, a reason
        the couple was making love

   your eyes
first time hit were demonic dishes

  bright stone to stone
& what was the reason now the couple
            we
making love

a riddle:
who burns
 closest to home?

    never exhausted
but close
 in not guessed

another coda:

his altar in a twined rune
twigs in the picture

the tables are dark
the time is auspicious
go my dream

before
pedestal of him

    bow vulnerable

(knees)
  under sign of Capricorn

Dallas

I tried to sleep and not doing that the night before the things I could tell you I come cloudy off the airplane my mind is clouded. And of you, too, obscured. I'm here to steal some entrepreneurial scenes, here to revoke some statements made in haste an earlier time before an agenda was set, the lights went out, before I even thought to resist abdication. An imaginative identification with the eccentric base of design. Technology hastens entropy. I speak to you in analogies. I am my subject: Dallas, and that is always the place, the scent of the dream. Don't manipulate the dragon, don't spoil the night ahead of us, the calm runway that leads back to what kind of city is it, is your fancy? Fancy, yet restrained by whatever does dry up. A used-to-be watering hole, and for the sense, a new suggestion of boom and push, a quality of self-reliance got us all here one time to make something new. Living in the enchanted domain as habitual creatures that long, although we deny it, for air. Is every sentence in order as it is? Did someone think this up and forget the example you too might provide. One's eye travels to the sky as more land. And land is of value especially as gratified desire is replaced by land. Land of no return. Landed emigrants who built it up. Land poor, land solvent. Land, you are never mine. And you who thought to land me, I landed here, out of reach. Touch the sky. Three strands of pearls adorn my neck, some resemblance to Coco Chanel, whose sweater jacket made her famous. A long time ago. A long time ago: dotted black veil over the eyes. My eyes being pools for the cameras to wade into. Come closer, come closer, I beckon you, mirrors of hope or fear. Restore my ascendancy, my classic cigarette. Come inside me as artifice. I'm not even of the generation that put this together, shucks, and turn away. I won't wear the hat of cowgirls or boots o' Spanish leather. I will stand beknownst to your ink stilettos of aggression and quick rage. Retained as heroine who won't take no for an answer. Answer not an engagement to be *nouveau riche* in a boom town, but it helps pay bills over the other side of the tracks. I had this writing in mind to be a current event, and tell you, even you, of atmosphere: roots and lucre. How American one can get in spite of lenient mix? Oil and property drink with the women as we listen to home-down music as trend expression of sex to get, to grab those burly men of sweat and cow fun. What isn't said with all the drawl of paradise, what isn't mustered with the ploy of glitter and shotgun, what results in solo night replaying the band you love the most, and take in the drug: bravado and release. Don't tempt me. What isn't stated in the Night Ruler manual, what isn't released in the fact-finding commission's report, what isn't resounding in your ears, what isn't lost in a mistake to distinguish how words are embedded in any given picture, is this:

They come apart   :   what isn't locked in pictorial space
They come apart   :   a clue to contemporary landscape
The Mexican mosaic :   it comes apart

What isn't known is the difference between a Saint's name and an eatery. Words are labels first, motifs second. Translations? The threat of losing conversation exacerbated here as you land. Your clothing demands labels, all the shops and merchandise are named. Almost inhabitable, the way we are living inside it, a city real enough to place confidence in. They come apart. Off-axis positions can't hold them. They are apart, counter to what we read, if we do read. Dallas, as given, specifies the terms of an encounter with a place, giving you directions for dreaming it. The verbal ones, or the suggested one. You arrived here, say to my assassinated selves, isn't it so? And you determine your context as an entire image might. Listen to the fragmented buildings and the decorum of traffic getting somewhere.

Aletheia

Aletheia is nothing mortal, as little as death itself.
—MARTIN HEIDEGGER

In the beginning of my tuning, in the act of tinkling a syllable and comically enjambing noise, I find a proper human song in Aletheia. She accompanies the sweetest turn of mind. She is the "Unconcealed," the she who grants the stage to whoever you want her to be. And you are night for her and you are a representation of her wish to be here fully clothed or be here fully naked, exhumed. And you are always night to her as you chatter in the day. What's the truth of Aletheia? She's your other, she's your challenge. You call them dulcimers? In the beginning: a syllable with her name inscribed on it. What's the truth in that? Burdens of folk appear with baskets of real things in time. Yet what they inhabit is choice spot of selling and consuming. The market place is bleak without them and they appear real. They cajole you with some exotic sex toy, or mini-skull in a filigree box. "This one, Madam?" She proffers the dried cube of mammoth flesh. You had hoped for something fresh and nourishing. You get the mixture of past horror and seduction. You recoil with your eyes that seek relief alighting on the face of a meek child. She has the delicate almond eyes of another race but is transforming too into the hag life, Aletheia again in any form. She's your other, she's your challenge. Give up fixation, keep walking, your mind mixing with syllables does all this. Its eyes are tentacles towards relief. Relief is the exposure of her scheme. She wants you to be happy. Relief is that carbon monoxide won't get you tonight. Go truly "underground." It is a relief to have tried hiding in her body. Relief is remote and anonymous behind dark glasses. You look like a soldier in your relief. She is a bunch of tanks in her loyalty. She's the martial type at 4 a.m. Aletheia has a feminine dreaminess about some of her boy fantasies. Her Colonel is beautiful. A relief is a young night flier who sleeps all morning in her arms. Aletheia stalks women. Aletheia knows the surgical language, phrases like "scarlet Mercurochrome." She gets you at the apex of your relief every time. Relief is her method and is the untuning of her strings. I heard her. I hear her. I hear her now. I hear her in my writing and by my window. I heard her yesterday as I walked back toward the disaster shops and panicky Mall. As I walked forward toward her insistence on meeting me there. I hear her. I heard her. I was once hearing her long ago, we're both children out under a lattice. Behind a lattice. Dear Aletheia: please position me properly in your recollection too. Is she a Tartar? Do I recognize the boot? Fur? Can she dance? Certainly. And is a certain success at whatever she chooses. Relief is a mastery to her and not swept aside, out on the street again. She flips a switch. Aletheia has Lethe in her name and if you go inside it you will meet something forgotten there. That is the scheme: to get you inside her. I go inside and meet my forgotten ladder, my trustworthy father, my small bed. I meet my dimple, my lips, my only son. I meet the ambassador I always wanted to replace. I observe his shoes. I meet the voice from the radio. I meet the sister of a man I will marry. I meet someone at the restaurant across my tracks. Aletheia has some cunning as she wishes to meet fame in my words of her. She is a scant truth, she is a hair's breadth away from it. In a philosopher's scheme she is all I could ask for. She gives orders. She obeys them. She forgets to acknowledge what in herself she has forgotten. That she forgets is not unusual. It brings me together with her. She lies down with the bear, with the buck, with the stallion, with the lamb. That she will be anything I command her to be as I meet her here is not something to hold against her. She is the plan of a virgin. One time I thought I could get ahead of corporate time by flying to Tokyo but she met me there, bargaining for stock. I was traded back. My stock went down. Our fertile meetings subsided. She kept upstaging me.

Fait Accompli

Look down. Heavier now. Onus of observable spectrums. A woman's body resounds. It waxes. It wanes. It hoards ammunition. It turns into something unrecognizable. O alas. My lights are not what they are monitored to bide in. They are mercantile and elegant prey. Subsist on the inward motion of laborious practices. Genitalia. Are you men or women hiding behind screens, behind veils. A stricter practice. And the Arab inside is a kind of knight in armor or old Protestant crawling to get into secondary light. Rides a secret channel not unlike a flashlight beams its arrogant ray upon you. Hide, hide from your own lipsticked face. Then consider what it is you recoil from. Politics if such a hinge exists in a random universe. Alive & still. Not to depress my native eyeballs but understand how such a game exists called back to roost already warmed over nihilism. Get up & out or spake as the male Messiah doth. Back again to bid time trumpet you are already born and dead Hosha'na! ("save us"). Compassion hath a note in here. What's wrong to take a hand shake a hand & kiss the lady when she's down. On the other hand: morbid, oblique, tired of waiting for guns to go off (please never go off). Writing you from a foxhole way down under under a moonless desert. Would-be lady scholar get your cerebrum out here. Respond or something to that effect what means are required what tableaux vivants. What are the taboos around here? Do not swear at the higher powers & keep your suffering to yourself. Are you cohabited with desire to change a version of the world? Seasonal displays are mounted. I heard Frankie Boy warbling in a lobby in Detroit decked with pine & pink satin bows. I heard high soprano "Noel notes" careening down an even longer corridor like a scream. The language turned harsh. Neighbors light a menorah. The newspaper says Muslims are on the move and we do not care as a populace, "to discuss religion." I meant but it's a threat but it's a fret but confusion is like the street. It's a wrecker, America: been out there lately?

Cabal

New green life is pricking the tussle
awake to tense melodrama. Veined
impressions come briskly out a keen
mind to discover exactly how truth
is figured. They're so preemptory
down there, I get speculative and
wonder what happened to invest their
minds with legends of garbled lore,
who did what to whom, part timorous
part sullen, try huge tips to the
hierarchy to no avail, or maybe that's
what they think I do. Let them let
it break out in small tongues. If you
break, break now, they say cynically,
who only wait and stand. Seeing nothing
from this point of view would be more
dangerous than a move from linked and
brutal continuity up a canyon.
It's endless scrutiny, characteristic
of the Age but without the sweet
agitation of Empress Eifuku, for
example, which to conceal excesses
demands you be there an early literary
life. The jag of books we had it,
baffling and capable, now vanished
in the past. Never acquired or fancy
money, not really evolved, rather like
momentum extolling events in a wider
season such as nocturnal desire and the
passion of a sleeve. Living on the street,
that was it, or something like it.
Assurance was frequent because you were fast
to what happens. Apperception includes
the feeling of life you were building

giddy in the morning, can't figure why.
Then rays became rods so dangerous that
suddenly Nature the way you love it is
acutely beautiful turning crimson and
man-made forests into something deadly
but never like true forests of stars
above your head, and you who also know
this, decide for yourselves. Anguish
you couldn't tell one night, or betrayal
if we really studied it, have made the
latest news of phonological and semantic
structures different. Language taking
over I can't say, but it's radical to be
unchanged in color, all the world with
lights and warnings, theirs too,
flowing with song, meaning the sequence
was modeled on parts not always whole.
Yet notes are joy, are healing, are heard.
Dear Male Poets: I enclose a leaf
and make you see insistence is human.
Or I point to indigenous spirits and
the like, angry spirits if you want to
talk about ancient infusions. Sadness
in religion is surrounding what you
represent. Turn it back. White hair
is brown again, wrinkles smooth to silk
and a dead eye sparkles. Adults are
children like you. Never arrested they
love inhabiting buildings all shapes
and sizes, and being attached to illusion,
darken the rooms with inclement behavior,
cajoling me again now and then,
jilted in the latest cabal.

Net Life

Insects, larvae, the mesh of forms. Net life.
Small as what could be a little village
Scene: rot, die, begin again
No, it's the familiar personal components
or rage, tossing back Grecian curls, didn't get
"the how much you get from the old man"
In winter still moving despite traffic, despite trees
You are not a street upstaging yourself
I'll tell you about modernity, & these trees
will glorify your ancestors carefully against the day
Make a pause avoiding collision
It's far from the continent, the oceans, the sky
What taste, O satisfied sleeper? Breath from your mouth
flags me down, my legs wobble on the stones
Walking, what is it you want, another tour de force?
I'm with you in the illusionist's boxes
Remembered boxes? Which are they? Take me back:
cologne, the bed, awkward stoical private radio,
Zurich, alone with your letter now, touch the words
Take me back: you know what I'll be saying
In time, in time I'm saying. The letter crepitates
in my pocket lining. The walking thigh.
Arming you in lace across my vision. A way across
my vision. The urge is on me to lie down, forget you
& sleep. Are you bright tonight? Fringed? Winged?
I scramble going for the easy pleasure. Aren't you.

2.

Tyrannical hold on German lyric is another net.
Some felt this century apart to tell you a storm close by
First light, flash loudly. Calling like in its element

those tribes. Now buried in the fetal position
Basalt, copper. Midnight bisects two years two days
Two lives, one person. And may or may not be
drinking: ambrosia, Pernod, ejaculate, laugh
a scribe who's as insistently complex as capillary
veins or the topology of anywhere stretched & dark
Some rug out from where it hurts & the present
provides details of organization, semantics, I do
vaunt. You think you find peace? Go about barefoot,
a grassy season, go about the curve in the road
I take the curve in your back. Go ahead.
On European earth trees take a chance
My name, a net, comes to end among familiars
Ask no more. My body, a net, ask no more, but say
about the day "It's Sunday, again, a mesh of forms"

Wide Receiver

You are designated "wide receiver"
  What works for fighting team works in me,
    in passing—*stella mare*—so that you are guiding light
    in battle, in morphology of landscape
      What field to dance upon?
        Human time, resistance to invasion,
          genetic mess, American largesse excused?

What made me large, breaking body down
  to a closer scrimmage? What field?
    It is trembling, it is near-body-down
    breaks, stymied, is the closer you are
      in your golden shining numbers,
        glinting armor, helmets, visors
          —down, down. Body hits pay dirt, down

To any line of thought, breaks occur to
  split into smaller increments
    of speech of touch, under classic poise, and finer
    than even the way sound operates in marrow
      could be, could be, could be oracular or
        muscular, war-like, expensive, stretched to a max
          & shouting a club song: Yo! Heh! Yo, dude!

Block & tackle? stick & stone? Could be
  warp & ride, or slow down, what team was it—
    not a national one not ethnically bound it's hoped—
    tied a body down to a name of origin, or dialect
      forebearers wore, a ribbon of color, or dialect
        that shows you might bow to an alien god, show
        you were cut at birth, a male thing to speak to

And you stand revealed as they tie you down,
  desecrate your sex, mutilate your bones
    they set you on fire to make a nationalistic point
      What captain of what team are you, what terror
        could you ever be? What game could ever
          not do you in? could never not kill your heart?
            Where could you ever go without riot & grief?

You are named, numbered, destroyed
  And what of the women on other side?
    Flip channel spectacle to shame our wave
      News? these old atavistic wars . . . cutthroat wars
        where women get mangled by hordes of barbarian
          mind-sets programmed to kill "other," "she," kill
            "other," "she," kill "she" in mantra-death chant

What feminine cheer could lead the anguished swell
  of hand-off from quarterback to running back?
    loathing of anything that does not carry same origin
      What wreaks havoc on the plains, in the desert
        what mind to rape before the walls of city, village
          ditch somewhere how low how low to go down
            low low low to go down down how low

War-machine-player face your loathing of the details of
  another one, take them away, swipe them, gun them down:
    the curve of chin, the colored cloth she wore, you hate it
      because it sings, plunderer, it reeks of "other"
        You hate the beauty that isn't yours, murderer
          you hate it because it is a different milk
            —yak or goat—from theirs

One would worship a graven image, another would
  slay the cow as in the colonial nightmare she dreamed of
    Was it so swift in coming? The reprisals?
      Occupied zones of horrific control quick to arrive?
        hell realms, fiery bardos, chill winds, rivers of ice, what shrine
          do you sacrifice these bloody bodies to? What goddess
            welcomes tortured breasts, severed heads?

Who crosses the line to win the proverbial dumbshow
  for now you turn off the sound & watch images of light
    float across an incomprehensible screen
      You wanna crack a beer? it's foaming on that screen
        you wanna make out on the sofa? Yo!
          you wanna get a new car & drive the open road
            You want to tally some ranks & scores?

Swift as thought for I thought this
  as I was thinking that thought that thought itself
    is deceptive for it thinks itself clever
      to be able to see differences, to be able to
        discriminate this torture, so pampered
          & educated and conditioned and "mental"
            from that one—the palpable suffering

Don't think when I said "calves of the athlete"
  that I wasn't thinking poetically, or
    "chest of the athlete" that I wasn't excited,
      or "tense muscles in the neck of the athlete"
        that I could be only pristine & disengaged
          He is shining in his sweat now, he is both
            gladiator & victim, he is a gorgeous male feast

To think upon not about sex—his torque & twist—
  but prowess, men on top of men, entwined
    and it is a sacrifice, & that guy thought he had it too soon
      crossing the line got tagged for arrogance,
        Was a running thought I had, saw him make a pass
          thought of argument & one fell and one just up & walked away
            now cheer you could surely cheer for him, it's over

208

Set your mind in the cauldron of flame,
  crucible of claustrophobic desire
    Decimate this other that steals in the night to take your shadow
      your gold your lover your words, that steals your sense &
        you go babbling, you go bonkers, tear off the helmet
          How to live in this cushy playground, Minerva
            What about the unknown risk O wounded Achilles . . .

Do these guys dream the unknown, an offensive penetration?
  Only 5 percent of the ocean floor is mapped, after all,
    so what do you say to that volcanic monopoly
      what tremor makes you tremble, how
        prepared is the question of any involuntary reply
          and how it affects your climates
            for this will be important in the days to come

Which come rapidly now & die harder each
  day, and what about the long-since-
    vanquished herbivores hunted by men—proto ancestors—
      who made camps by vanished lakes, springs, streams
        Where are they in a history I can't
          begin to fathom because it smacks of such
            pecuniary impurity, poesy's preternatural doom

Those were the better days, but were they my friends?
  In this sermon which says itself, repeats hoping
    to impress the crowd for what is poetry but for
      to reach you, my friends, my friends
        O those were the days & those were the days
          my friends my friends and now it's sport & war
            & violent sins 'gainst women & nature

Identify the enemy that stalks her hallway
   Reconvergence now, filling the pages of earth
      with words of a section of the newspaper made over in
         whose recalcitrant image, of one maimed & mainstream?
      In this sermon one does as in a sermon preach
         to you who are Yes!—converted already
            who are the audience to tableaux of violent bondage

And discipline, raging now to be held
   accountable: to score to win to grow to prosper
      to score to win to grow to prosper (& this is the oral part)
         to abound to set the world on fire to take it to
            the top to the top to the top take it to the top
               where all the old scores settle, then churn again—
               HIKE!

Lokapala

dedicated to the Nelumbium speciosum
(lotus)
which closes
towards evening

and to

Indra
Agni
Yama
Surya
Varuna
Parvana
Kubera
Soma

Lokapalas all

LOKAPALA: A NOTE

*When you have exhausted your power, a conquer-the-world-is-at-your-call
mentality and hit the ground (bottom), you meet Lokapala who al
ways resides there. She is what we'd strive for, or he as the case may
be, or both to confront and subsume. Absorb. It's what the great reli-
gions attempt all the time & often Lokapala eludes them. The black
Madonna of Chartres hides under Christian guise but secret fertility
goddess still reigns in her niche. Supreme and sublime. Her spot was
consecrated long before the masons arrive, or glass cutters begin their
magnificent inspiration to conjure religious images (see the devils re-
side there?) creating an effect to admire and worship. They saw light
through the colorful shadows of a transcendent dream: molecular,
splendid conjunctions of line, pattern: in what cortext do they dwell?
But couldn't help but honor her, the matrix of the dream, alive in
glass. Loka is place or realm. Pala, the protector of that spot. Trees*

*are lokapalas, as are rocks. This is choiceless. Humans try to become
famous in home towns or Stonewall Jackson in battle. You died
miles away in combat and return to a cheering plaza. It's natural.
You could name a figure of speech or someone otherwise attached to
locus. We say "The Spirit of St. Louis," we say "Our Lady of Guada-
lupe," the same virgin who appeared to Juan Diego a converted In-
dian on a site sacred to the mother goddess Tonantzin. It embodies
the act of recognizing, naming and meeting the deity (yourself?) on
the spot. Deities are like animals who unleash a scent to claim a
neck of the woods or corner of the house. They are fierce protectors
and you must appease, cajole, flatter them and supplicate their mercy
to abide wherever it is you encounter them (in dreams, in mirrors as
well). They never sleep. They are always "on guard." They might
dwell around bridges like Billy Goat's Gruff. The realtor understands
this, the landlord too. This poem is meant to be danced in simple
postures of gesture and ownership. Stomping but not moving the feet
from one spot is recommended. Get down on haunches, squat. Or in
lotus posture, set your roots down. Gravitate to the center of the
earth. Held by gravity, and like a plumb line, you traject to the heart
of the universe. But Lokapala is jealous of any usurper. She's got a
turf to mark out and command. She inhabits the place you've always
longed for, but unlike you, she has no choice and you get envious of
her choicelessness. She "comes with the place." It is a force field and
a state of desire, like the wind always starts up in the same place. A
sacral dance of both possessiveness and longing: can you perform
this? I have tamed the place and the feeling is mutual. To be tamed
in a just reciprocity is the only clue to how it works. But you must
pay homage in an appropriate manner. Bow? Ablutions? Offer gold?
The room I write this note in was a room the mother was dying in &
the same room I wrote poems one late August: a room I dwelled in
constantly for a time, refuge and power spot. I could close the door.
The house the room sits in is placed on the artery of a small town
bypassed by the Erie Canal. The geomancy is not always clear. I
wrote then as I write now in a stupefied state of awe for magic of
place, of atmosphere. Where does it arise and how many factors go
into maintaining an hallucination? You can drown out the responsi-
bility sometimes with an obstruction, with an edifice that resembles*

every other edifice. And in Guatemala the corn gods and goddesses go
further underground to survive. No one strokes their silken locks now.
The intruders were strong. They raped the most beautiful places,
made them bend to a macho will. And always the aggressors will be
haunted by the shapes under the soil who strike back at the appropri-
ate time. You spoke of presences last night? You said you felt them?
One was just a blue light in a dark bush? Lokapala is available for
cohabitation on her own terms. It's how you will enter with body,
speech, and mind. She will cohabit with your eyes, your ears, your
nose, your tongue. She will press up against you. And even if you
think you've conquered her, and although she might slip away "fur-
ther back," like a lover she will never simply walk away.

Cherry Valley, N.Y.
Thanksgiving, 1990

LOKAPALA

1
BODY

Placed here
feet on ground
Place is here
Here's the ground
Here's earth repeating itself
Stake it out
Place to be of
I place what I know of it
& of this me all particles
Inside me
on the ground
All particles assemble
to be earth witness
Feet sink into place
Place bound by river
bound by mountain

by magic forest bound
by consummate ocean bound
I'm placed under sky
on globe dot
Body place is dot
& takes up edges of rocks
Makes up a shadow
is dot to take up space
is body dot, is micro dot
See it activate above plains
in passionate gesture
of decision road swerves
Road swings
Body walks to refresh limbs
limbs swing
Breath draws in
self-secluding dot
Draw the world in here
Body on ground
sits down on spirits
of plants & rocks
Spirits placed here
to command place
Lokapala placed to rule
To magnetize rain to this place
Catch sun here
(But is night coming?
Is she coming yet?)
Command the distance
from a star point
to imprint on body dot here
Placed here to rule
to name itself
The form takes its place
to embody insights
of seeds & ferns
calcite & bone

to gather all the shards
of a virgin world
all shards of an
explicative world
Pulverize broken bits here
Locate spur of timbre here
all sounds of things placed
here to rule
Gather here to
witness command
Place for body
to be prodded by warmth
Place to magnetize fuel
Keep moving keep moving
Is she here yet?
Is she coming?
You are noticed here
with warm body
expelling heat
expands to a finite universe
Keep burning
Keep burning here
Keep alive the one spot
Flames roll
I make an anvil
for this place
I forge out of this earth
metabolic night
I keep to my cave
(Is she coming?
Is she coming yet?)
I'll be the vigilant one
All night long
I keep to my spot
Command daylight here
Wait for night
Metabolism located

in a busy dot
got activated here
surrounded by alligators
surrounded by armies
You thought you could trick me
off my raft!
Trick me out of my armies
survey the scene ahead
& count me out
I am located in the
bend in the road
located on the tip
of her tongue
hidden in the weapon's point
decend into Dakshun Kali's
womb-grotto
where I serve her
as a rock might
a platform from which
to command
located like a command
performance
like a need to balance
day & night
located like a champion
on the 10th floor
located inside the beast's belly
placed here to inhabit place
marked out by augurs
placed to the mountain
adjacent to a path of burrs
prickly in moonlight
off a hidden moon
Walking to horse trough
inhabiting the drip
inhabiting your back
inhabiting your hand

Live inside the gorse
gruff weeds
live inside glistening prophecy
inside the need to pacify
He wants to go to the front,
my buddy does
But I'll stay here
inside the front
live inside
but always facing forward
ready to act
toward the street
First sheltered in a hutch
then homeless
exposed to elements
Refusal to be deprived
of the refusal of the enigmatic
Power increases as I gather
forces here
things-in-themselves
as witness here
to stake out my claim
My spot
Placed inside the weapon
my spot I claim
as sport
to spin here as challenger
large, desperate, waiting
to ensnare you
Wondering at the precise
time of invasion
Afraid to be trampled
by alien powers
To be stomped on
None of that!
(Is she here yet?
Is she really coming?)

I belong here
in my fear of being invaded
I protect the spot
as margin of disbelief
as margin of accomplishment
under the floor
ghost! ghost!
under the floorboards
Hear it? I say
"ghost! ghost!"
Haunts the place
inside a body to be
spent in battle yet?
Is she coming yet?
Protect the avenue for her
Place located at the adagio
placed inside a body strategically
to defend a spot
to mark it out by augury
Task in the dark
inhabiting a close shave
Protecting you
protecting the region
A point of view
my position is fixed
The longitude & latitude
is cited
No advantage but to stay
Frighten you
with my stubbornness
until you honor my presence
You stumble here
recruiting all the power I have
Protecting the years
The land is tamed
How many throws of the dice?
How many lovers made love here?

(Is she here yet? Is night coming?)
Night descend once more
to this ground of passion
Stomp on this place to be
a fortress
I'm vigilant
with eyes of the condor
& fast like wind
located like night is everywhere
everywhere
Guard my zone of control
Conquer with my seductive arm
Lean back

2
SPEECH

Speech is intimate
like a place inside you
comes out to be located
Outside you
placed in the accordance
of breath with desire
Place located inside your mouth
cradled by tongue
Pushed out
or propelled towards
all of you
Spoken on the tongue
Shout: Heh   Heh
Ha   Ha
Ho   Ho
Hoo
Guard well your tongue
Spit speech, gut it out
Bite down mouth
Lacerated from too much

219

too much speech!
speech lacerated
in standing here
A fool to read a newspaper standing here
Is morning here
(Is the morning, the news
here yet?
Has it come? The news?)
Speech located in love of boy
or lot of tamed land
herbs growing here
Speak: EH   AH   A   U
Located in the love of news
In hearing delicate sounds
of EEE   OOOO
Woo   Woo   Woo
New words or
punctuation come out
a grammar of light or rant
Or dent these words into speech
with the imprint of desire
They'll speak for you
You said "punch"
You said it was a
punch, it was
You said how words
could change a language
Inside a speech of an Irishman,
"punch" it was
a lilt or sweet slur
which is a shape of syllables
& they have buzzing colors
and they have buzzing colors too of
sigh or grunt
or song sonorities
or stress to press against the meaning
interpreted here

of eye to ear or ear to eye
hands off
glissando's symmetry
The voice will spell & snarl
or swell bursting the heart
Utterance is the place to
start a day's push
against the air to articulate
the closer you are
to place
Placed here to drive home
the salient point
& point underneath
the tree for the root
of alphabet
The protector of speech
has a loud mouth
composing also beautiful poems
to keep you grounded
Speech of family or home
wants tempering
the tax speech is difficult
also speech of your panic
Relocate to another text
come out, come out
come out again
ghost! ghost!
Come out to be located in desire
in desire
Come out to be counted
Vote, be recognized
Say your piece
Come out to say Yea or Nay
to march with your slogan
to kneel in midday
chanting your prayer to
a voice unseen

221

to say I do this
I do that
so that your place
(in body) is
verbal presence of mind
To state yourself here
& stake out
the preamble & conversation
& converse with the spirits
of place
say their names
organize their seed syllables
Invite them to the dance
Question them
How many centuries have you
tarried there
What is the secret spell
to activate your spot
What sound charms your heart?
In whose service
are you manifest?
What is the song
to sing at dawn
What midday
What at night?
Is your preference
wooden instruments
or those of metal
and clay?
Do you call her back?
How? And will she come
Is she coming, is she coming
yet? Night? Yet?
What is your favorite name
and how do you name yourself
when your shape changes
Have you the voice of

a child?
Will you hear us if
we call?
Are we doomed to the
company of human voices
or may we speak to dragons?
Can you hear it
ghost! ghost?
What is the specter
of death here
Will it sing?
Is place an odyssey
Is the dot you locate
from in the center of your
forehead, your throat
your heart
Do you want to be obeyed?
Are you ready to be overtaken
Has war been declared
Have the armies stopped speaking
to one another
What is the sound of desert
covered with battle & blood?
Whose corner will you occupy?
How long does it take before
speech occurs
come out! come out!
News come out!
What happens?
What is happening
in the border tribes
Talk again
Conquer with your tongue

3
MIND

Mind of spectral places
Mind overcast like day
It begins
Channels move out of my house
like rays of mad dogs
to find their place
Your mind. Is it your mind?
The mind that woos & speaks
is located in the animal this moment
in Molly's cry the next
Mind gives up on a magazine
Mind motions back to the beginning
Mother mind, are you there?
How it starts, is triggered
by a glance
starts up, kicks in
to acknowledge
place in body
goads on & sports with the notice
got a body
with limbs
dances inside this form
is encapsulated by it
Romance to make it solid
& be in love
or in hate (dented)
then breaks apart
& is of many minds
Goes mad
splitting & branching off
Notice the sweat on the brow
of her mind
She's been observed
in concentration on a minute thing

How the edges of her moisture
light up
She sweeps her hand
across her forehead
like a soldier is hot
in battle
in the jungle
Mind in place—can that be said?
How can you say that?
Is it upon us?
The flood? a great melting?
Is it coming, the great drying up?
Desert?
Have the armies crossed the
imagined line yet?
Is it to be thought of?
Will they make it?
Has she marched in yet
with her many wide battalions?
Will she stomp her feet there?
Can we rescue this place from
scorch & burn?
Can you speak of it or are
you just thinking
How can you say "is mind in place"?
Does it have a chance?
She is formidable
I piped my mind
into the pipe in the range
of old time & talk
Mind in spectral places
Mind overcast like the day began
The channels move out like rays
You say this again because
it describes the action
the little tunnels witness
as mind travels through

The yardmen approach
with a plan
To lay more pipe & channel
water through
Looking over the distance
get up close to the board
"This is the spot"
They say
"This is it, this
is the spot"
"But how wide?"
"How wide is it?"
Try a plan
Put your mind to it
& birds & humming too
Try it
Get a mind focused on the
spark of weapon's point
on knife that cuts night
(Is she arrived yet?)
Get a mind hooked to
a syllable resembling
a picture of standing awe
that stands awake
electrifying blue
Syllable that echoes
your response
& turns a pulse
Light beats down
on the definitive town
on the definitive brick
recognized by itself as
a kind of torch
beacon of what could occur
what could be built
what could light a way
To be home to

be a layer
over the spot you selected
when you last looked
(*Lokapala was waiting*)
So many explosions inside a cone
inside the calling inside
concept "town"
budding in a kind of
trance preparation
because mind is golden
like the Aztec city
mind lifts the wind like
a sacrifice
mind is heart exploded
O believe it
a particular blush or blurt
It's semi-arisen
It cropped up because
it can't help exuberance
& leads the way toward
slam or dunk
through hoop of mind
O believe it
My spot spoke loudly to me
as soldier or good sport
Lost its quick attire
long expanse to go a
billion light-years
waiting for any dream
to poke you out
sighting her / my past
to clinch it
Where does mind come from?
It's all mental now
traces of wounds disappear
at twilight
(*she's coming, she's*

coming soon, now)
Healed, yet aging
The mind knows more now
that it's collected
other points of view
& politics were soundly dressed
over in a current mood
As fuel got spent, got
spent, got spent
& mind won't take too much
to go on
It goes on
So is she here yet?
May I call her back if
I have to?
Will she come?
She is revelatory
in her posture
in her look of animal intensity
to guard her spot
Is she the lost animal
in my desire?
What is mind's desire?
Do the parts add up
Is the picture well-rounded
Do the women meet their bodies
first inside the belly of
their own minds
Questions are thoughts too
The coiled syllable stretches
As you watch it it weaves
vibrating through
the channels of life & death
Could I say more?
That the place is forbidden
That that is why you go there
That you were located

in the curiosity
that jumped first
that leaped to
seize on that spot
or thought
That you spoke cruel things
all around
That speech lead you to war
That mind could never
fully be spoken
Mind was coiled
& waiting
Outer, inner
& secret latitudes
could map
the touch of mind
It is a torch to
the deity
who lies coiled
& waiting
that asks *are you
here yet*
that stole your mind
one day
that tripped your wire
& you fell back
into concept
It was a ruse to
shed a tear
on this very ground
on which you began
to grow
Here's earth
Stake it out

Noösphere>>>>>>>>>>>>>>>>>>>>

Literally we're saying here the *head* sphere—I'll basically take on the head sphere. I have an over-active head, a beating mind. "Noösphere" is Pierre Teilhard de Chardin's term, Chardin a Catholic priest cum Gurdjieffian, working 20's, 30's, the first Catholic priest to accept evolution, he studied layers upon layers, the stages of the emergence of life. Noösphere: the consciousness sphere. The mind is connected to life, biosphere. You know Niels Bohr's one possible theory that things come into existence only when we look at them? Or Bishop Berkeley's "esse est percipi?" Or Blake's "the eye altering alters all"? Animals, insects will see the whole picture quite differently. But we have our mental habit. *We see what we want to see.* "Things exist, like the echo of our voice at the foot of a mountain" (Ikkyu). Wherever you look the disturbed mind will be everywhere, the unbalanced mind will be there & everywhere. Everyone will have it. It's no mystery. Perhaps it's very simple. As humans we have a very high level of consciousness equally packaged with ignorance. Not ignorance of not knowing, but of wrong knowing.

And yet the nature of reality is something that can't be changed & can't be manufactured by concept or philosophical speculation. The nature of reality is finally without watcher; it doesn't require anyone to observe or look at it. In other words, we could say reality is unconditional. The nature of reality is free from observation, therefore it can't be spoken of in conventional words. It can, however, be experienced. Poetry, sacred writing gets close. How do we then begin to understand the **samsarodadhi**—or ocean-like world? How do we write it? Why would we want to? What is our watcher habit? Where is our guardian habit? How do we protect ourselves from ourselves? Why have we created such a version of reality? Why have we been so cruel? Why is it we no longer really need nature to experience anything? We're still dependent on nature for food but we rarely get the connection. When Gary Snyder asked me in the early 70's where my water in Lower East

Side Manhattan came from I glibly said out of the tap of course. My son & his friends complain if they have to WALK anywhere. And yet they, the children, think "money grows on trees." Nature poets are viewed with cynicism because they seem to need to make themselves feel sensitive by responding to a pretty sunset, a wilted flower. Ted Berrigan cynically couldn't be out in nature because it no longer gave him ideas for poems. Yet the nature vocabulary could be used, cannibalized. But would you honor & bow to the thing itself? Whereas in the city your mind could go in 10 directions at least. When I asked a Buddhist lama about moving out of the city early 70's, going "country" like people were doing, back to land, he said No you stay in New York, work on New York, it's a holy city. You have to transmute it, he said. What a tall order. Intoxicated, I could see all the wires in my walls as veins of some maniacal beast that had its network, its tentacles everywhere. I visualized grids of nerves & muscle & electricity of my city. My city had giant cockroaches parading down 2nd Avenue. My city was the nightmare & the dream. The noösphere was my mind racing to be synchronized with the pace of subway, to never be late. To be on time for the next human power meeting. Everything had a mindset of scheduling. One switch could throw the whole thing off. I read Dante to understand the nature of the plan. To understand the karma of hell. How we got to a place we couldn't even turn the corner in. I wrote down the words of madmen who stood underneath my window on St. Mark's Place howling at the skies. I wanted to meet my energy at the hub of the city, at the interstices of power. I wanted all the codes. I could see the concentric & intersecting cycles of life mainly human forms. The biosphere? I would taste the arctic world at Central Park zoo. I would find a patch of green somewhere. Intoxicated I studied for seeming hours the strange fleshy plant form at my feet as I meditated in the park, finally realizing it was my own Band-Aid I'd inadvertently abandoned. Later I'd visit the Biosphere project in Arizona, where you have an ideal beach with exotic pebbles flown in from state-of-the-art beaches & functioning ecosystems and a machine that keeps the water flushing its waves. And yet the people, the experimenters enclosed in that bubble were losing weight rapidly, turning pale. You can get into many of the prehistoric caves in Southern France, and experience the assimilated facsimiles. Lascaux. Does it matter if it's real? *The end of nature?* The end, even, of human nature? How can you glorify that seemingly gorgeous Rocky Mountain trail close to Colorado's Rocky Flats when you know how the plutonium has leaked into the streams running through it, giving rise to monstrous distortions, cancers of all kinds. Sheep born with three legs, no hair. Eyeless cows. We kill our animals then flaunt their skins. We are at odds with our animal natures. We no longer love the real animals our animal selves once communicated with. A Penguin man in a popular movie is deformed, vengeful, a dark wrathful angel who wants to destroy the firstborn of Gotham City. A man hides behind the mask of a bat but can't really fly. Catwoman is schizophrenic, her sexuality a timebomb, purring & hissing to explode. We still use animals to name our weaponry, showing how far our distortion will take us. My son writes stories from the point of view of insects which is at least a sympathetic, tender response. Taiwan calls its missiles Green Bee, Shy Horse. South America has its Condor I & II. We sent an Eagle to the moon. Mind is outer space. Ross Perot calls the members of his paramilitary operations Eagles. They stay in eyries, motel rooms, perched there to descend on the computers. From a notebook kept on recent travels:

> Sikh boy-child at
> airport
> holding
> plumes of peacock feathers—
> Pakistani?
> topknot rises up above the mysterious fan
> he makes pretending at an animal

> Sister
> in black
> embroidered dress
> pigtails, smiling . . .

peacocks & pigtails, luminous details in the Gatwick airport terminal night.

Because we have not made friends with our world, our selves, we Eurocentric predators are haunted by the beasts we destroy everywhere, we are haunted by the ghosts of Native Americans, and by the Afro-American slaves who were never named. They are our *other* nature. Our needed dark side. We have such a complicated need so they come back to us distorted. We name our cars after disappearing tribes, extinct animals. The words are substitutes, at great remove, with a lingering power that troubles us—faint whiffs of beauty & power of our misty & not so ancient past? We destroy what we love perhaps so we may finally own it in a perverse kind of translation. We are no longer troubled by its true existence. It doesn't take up so much space. What is this "we," white woman? I write these musings as poet trying to make sense of her world.

Grace of These Lacunae

= grew small in late afternoon =
= designed a garden =
= perjorative slap =
= middle years jolt me out =
= do you know color? =
= is it an elder green like you? =
= waiting on all women's lips =
= could the she be encountered or revealed? =
= why not =
= momentary sense of town problems =
= went forth to high places =
= stick in hand =
= ruffled some feathers, bloom =
= upon bloom, for it was spring =
= broke into laughter =
= pretending badly =
= other marks to infiltrate =
= or refrain from making =
= illustrations from a life =
= parents arrive =
= the odds are never theirs =
= I am a tomb-guardian =
= I guard the room of the father =
= as father, inspect the tableau =
= how did mother co-exist =
= garden . . . town . . . bloom =
= her room has its rumble =
= her room has its odor =
= his is the man's realm =
= fear & desire =

Lessons Shed Light

for Bobbie Louise Hawkins

Sanctity of text, devoted reader
whose syncretic pasttimes
trapped into obeisance
to page, how posit their
extensive imagination?
How explicate seduction?

Her lyric might be muted, infertile
but is she an instrument?
Yes, and a delicate one
redefining her own terms,
& ponders closely
Boccaccio's attitude toward text

Toward her sweet surface
they arise, happy further terms:
swoop, squirm, labor-intensive, cornice,
plague, probate, epigone,
more intense than any law . . .
pretense obscures the Aleph?

She writes all night . . . . She . . . .
but even thoughts less hard
are woven in with her study for
literary delights are her obsession
What is life with no
Dante, no Gita, no Cantos?

Read out like slats,
no puzzle no fester or blind
over master intent
but oral gauge & song soar then
on lissome kinetic waves
that melt into pleasure of kiss & book.

for Harry Smith

musicologist, alchemist, shaman, bookworm, filmmaker, archivist who
  kept his wits raging about him until his death the night before
  Thanksgiving 1991

we joke about running off to Thailand together
the big Buddha, the temple of a thousand desires
I will study the song, the flora the fauna
get stoned
you take your machines

"Buddhas are able to take the pain
because pain does not exist"

constant irritation
(it's worth it)

botched teeth
("Dr. Weber says they'll eat into my brain")

laugh at the end of the cigarette, menthol
but how many drags to finish that thought
a next con
arcana in the breeze
the last Navajo, the last Mohawk, Iroquois
stand in the shadow of

grinning corpse

I sat on the mushroom on the margins of the corporate world
record the sounds in the Bardo, Harry
speed you on the way

He heard coughing on the tape he recorded every time I said the
word "suffering" at the dharma talk   It came from the left side of
the room & mostly women

Forays to the Chelsea Hotel
to see you hold the demons at bay, cute wand, reels of tape
what goes on between those phonemes you note & experience
what pause, tick, jerk, pang, dwell here, smoke screen
what notch, twitch, tidbit, makeshift table, the chairs are always
    awkward
comfort is not the game, no hid place, no rest, live at the edge of a
    seat,
perch, blast, explore the radio, the small animals at the gate, push the
    button to hear the
ambience of any buddhafield, start tasting your own death, spit, nurse,
    subvert,
hug no one, pitch the door
light go out

& we stood, I remember distinctly at the corner of 12th & Ave A,
mucus running out of your mouth, it's winter, and I look into your eyes
mischievous as ever, what to do about you take you home with me?
You're going back you say to "record the sounds of dying men in the
men's shelter"

frail trickster
you won't wear the brand-new shirt from May D & F I bought you

Let it rot in hell a season

Thanksgiving
10 below you're starving, no food in the house
that kind of drink with calories for old people runs out
cats to feed
stumbling in snow to all-nite gas station for an eskimo bar
you let melt unable to chew

no such thing as inherited existent pain

if it existed inherently it would never leave

what you taught me:

genuine compassion:
seeing your friend having a nightmare

you know how it is real
& how it is not real too

dear Harry

the library is a secret

when will they find out?

the male deities return to dance
in a spiral
on the linoleum you say like a checkerboard

"I want it so boy Ambrose will come & play the human chess with
    me"

turn this mention upside down, the left-hand path
missing you in the dark ages, buddy

Last Rite

for Ambrose, Chloe, & Devin

We stop
    brother & I, his wife, our children,
    one cousin
to scatter father's ashes
     at the edge of Union Lake,

South Jersey
he sometime dwelled,
back,
   before a war,
  lineage's son of glass factory blowers
working hard in Protestant ethic

Sweet squall cooks up &
casts fine filaments of
  human powder, flinty bone
back into our eyes
see? see?

He was a gentle man, handsome
insomniacal, complex
 stubborn too
   glint of his
fleshly grit
come back—
    spec to haunt an eye

Jurassic

You'd think time had lost its way for you
You laughed before you thought this

Then earth rolled under wheel as
you drove across Route 80 blinded by sun

Putting on shades startled the Ute & Shoshone
(Jim Bridger settled later as the beaver trade dried up)

Muskets, bright feathers, phantom beadwork, bulldozers
Are all implements that turn the wheel

They speak to you as no other history does
Then you "cracked" the window to breathe fresh air

It adds up to a fraction of any life and yet
you are not the Dallas Cowboys, the Los Angeles Raiders, the Denver
    Broncos

You are not the Washington Redskins or New York Giants
(In the growing incredulity of these names)

You are She's-Driving-a-Car-on-a-Saturday
Observing a dirt truck kick up a mirage

You are moving down the incline too
Curious & smaller than the rest of the dinosaurs

Perhaps this is the last light you will ever see
Lining the beautiful earth

from Iovis, Book 2: Glyphs

"A scribe whose hand matches the mouth, he is indeed a scribe."
—SUMERIAN PROVERB

"Who shall read them?"
—JOHN L. STEPHENS

The poet is enamored of syllabaries, alphabets, the phonemes of any old tongue & groove. She travels to the Yucatán to meet a stubborn knowledge, secret, yet vibrant still in its actual display, the toil & play of its living people, their tragic dis-inheritance, and the ruins that bring her to her knees in awe & astonishment. Egypt's remnants, many moons back, were never quite like this to stop her mind. The closer continent intrigues the imagination more subtly perhaps? Less trampled? Unvoiced? Hidden? She moves with a scholarly companion of equal stamina & inquisitiveness. They read into the night on a humble cot one bare lighthulh outside Tulum, into Cobá, Valladolid, Chichén Itzá, Mani, Uxmal, Mérida always checking the simple rooms for reading bulbs & lamps. Reading old accounts by night, eye-balling incised glyphs by day. What sounds behind their fierce facade, what lore, what language, what action, what myth what passion ruled, how much warrior/slave blood spilled to meet a dire halluci-nated need? Who built what & how. She is sometimes Rabbit-Scribe. Sometimes, Mescal-Lady Great-Skull-Zero.

& the code
            public record stopped mid-sentence. . . .
        a great backbone of volcanoes
codes a mighty kinship
    & arrived there a kind of prod
        forgone conclusion
that it sounded in an ear,
        a jungle ear, serpent vision hiss

or strum, that it made sense,
              created a universe, a world tree
       a "raised up" tree: *Wacah Chan*
she goes down to market.............

       The priests want her thus placed,
conjunct to reality,
     hazed in the dream of sacrifice so that instead of
blood blood blood
it's star star star star

   the route of divinity crosses the firmament, the world goes out,
       eclipsed,
(fired) (see eclipse tables of Dresden Codex)
released or realize in the abstraction: it could go
on, the "let," the blood

& my dear friend, always in sight, throws light around
amongst the good skulls, a rude awakening to rend your flesh
off off
I learned all this from a skeletal woman
       reading the columns left to right
                       top to bottom
about twins & oppositions, metaphors for a concept of change
paddlers representing day & night

one thing replaces another replaces another replaces another
chan (caan) sky
& *chan (caan)* snake
a homophony, a glorious conjunct

nobody knows when it started

more arcana:
1. the database must be large enough, many lengthy texts
2. the language must be known, a reconstructed ancestral version.
   Linguistic family should be known.

3. a bilingual inscription of some sort is necessary
4. the cultural context should be known
5. for logographic scripts there should be pictorial references

Who can read the inscriptions under the bulls or elephants of Indus-
    Harappa?
Who shall read them?

forests hacked away
    what changes is not the will......Atlantis?
(Olson thinking this, off base, hunts among stones)
or astronomer tracks the skies, celestial tropical nights
  looks down, stares down the long stelae, complicated, in moonlight

The royal scribes write the data & deeds down in bark-paper books
devotees of the twin Monkey-Man gods
they live to write, lords of language
"linguistic boundaries leak like sieves"
but they mouth the lines linked to place, dark deed, lineages & destinies

(It is not possible in Mayan to use an imperfect verb (referring to ac-
tions or events in the past, present, or future that have not been com-
pleted) without sticking a date or temporal aspect adverb in front of it.)

buried a millennium.....
                        then

ghosts   should endure .... go on ....
    go on .... & walking
4 million Maya still walk these lands .... gone on ....
    gone on & walking
made it .... object .... ? .... this is play .... ? ....
    important
---------------unauthorized lives .... but gone on walking these lands
    .... incised
? .... or   wasted .... go   back .... it
written .... claw .... precisely .... that they
    walk, speaking .... what is memory?

243

hand on chin to visit .... get up to ask .... cut off ....
/////////////////////////
thinking .... thinking .... polished .... walking ....
  timely to walk the
sacbe .... disappointed ....
  come again .... it is a day time ? .... talk with friend ....
  drink *balche* ....
exchange ? .... happy? .... all parts & more .... feathers
  .... eat *keehel wah*........
breast plate/////////// ...... the day it was transcribed .... that was
  the house of .... changing lord
it is his name .... the name of fire .... name the lord of fire
  ....
he drilled fire .... the ballcourt .... watch .... it was the lintel
  that was his .... ? ....
memorial of the house .... ////////////----------------over------------------
& she went down to market & heard the news

various guises of Venus

It was a great ceremony, don't lose me here.

and of "Count" Jean Frederick Maximilien Waldeck (1766–1875), the
historian William H. Prescott (in a cutting Boston tone) once confided
to Mme. Fanny Calderón de la Barca: he "talks so big and so dogmat-
ically..... that I have the soupçon that he is a good deal of a charlatan."

producing drawings & architectural reconstructions fanciful in the
  extreme
he died of a stroke, pretty girl passing by .....
maintaining til the end of his life Maya civilization had been derived
from the Chaldeans, Phoenicians, and especially the "Hindoos"
what folly lurks there what coded racism?
(Lady Xoc nods, crouching before the Vision Serpent
in the year AD 681
& vomits up the future, all that will occur will occur)

one of a long line of fascinators, fascinated by, fascinated on, to
    "crack" it
what got coded long before you were born, the earth went dark & then
    they came
in .... Constantine Samuel Rafinesque, John Lloyd Stephens, Frederick
Catherwood, Alfred P. Maudslay, Teobert Maler, Charles Etienne,
Brasseur de Bourbourg, Ernst Forstemann, Leon de Rosny, Eduard
Seler, Cyrus Thomas, Desire Chamay, others, Thompson, Knorosov &
you, woman, what of your great quest? A bow to Linda Schele ...

Boleta de Entrada, and we go in
coded/closed..........................> > > > > > > > > > > > > > > > > > >
> > > > >open to?
                    feathers & arrows, the heavy plumage
lead off by the curve of a neck> > > > > > > > > > > > > > > >
> > >what Toltec sacrifice?

> >you play or
not> >

certain death

This is an assignment where you go to a museum to observe the past
    in a twist of fate
it is often the shape of bird (clay, bronze)
object made it of itself myself
that was itself a kind of death-rattle
(see *tzab*, the rattlesnake rattle resonates with the Pleiades)
but more objective, like removing the mind of . . .
but you say about the sacrifices, they go willingly, but a horror in the
    face
panic not the stupefaction, or seeing the vision, eyes wide
flowers, earrings, wool wrapped around an old lineage miles ago
& how important in my life? decked out . . .
slaves & bastard children, those who lost at ball

my clan? my kin?
what topology O proto-America

it was her way out
& then she whispered because she was speaking in me, a kind of Maya:
hallucinogenic bone tube enemas, they carry the vision into the stream

I cried I started I leap I strap down. Doctor Witch he came down on
me I go out I go out a light like she who might die in a short stretch,
flower cut *ex stasis*, this one Amazonian brazos. This old arm twisted
body burn she valiumed out like lights. See her Momma see her I go
get down the basement out the body now see me wizarded or wizened
a mother's thigh, she in *huipol* she in bright flowered sun, Mérida. A
dream, and then he came inside me, a shorter death . . . . . .

*In the evening we took another hot-bath at the lotería, and the next day
was Sunday, the last day of the fiesta, which opened in the morning with
grand mass in the church of San Cristóbal. The great church, the paint-
ings and altars, the burning of incense, the music, the imposing ceremo-
nies of the altar, and the kneeling figures, inspired, as they always do, if
not a religious, at least a solemn feeling; and, as on the occasion of grand
mass in the Cathedral on my first visit to Mérida, among the kneeling
figures of the women my eyes rested upon one with a black mantle over
her head, a prayer-book in her hand . . . .*

Mérida tall beauty, a bloody plan a wound dead never but state of
settled mind, unsettled, those descendents calibrated to spy on the af-
ternoon. Mérida, the helpful-panama-hat-man guides me to the post
office, then saves a parking space, illegal, going wrong way. Somber.
Hombre. Buying tequila Hornitos now to recompense a green mind.
The lover in his beauty, eyes bore into mine. Locked. Wanting to taste
the bitter lemon & salt of life. Then she goes down to market . . . .

dream: copal smoke rising like a snake
she goes down to market
all the Indians are silent

she goes down to market
in an awareness of earth, it is a clay musical instrument
& air brings sound & soul to the object
contact with an alien symbol, try again
(she weaves she weaves)
clay is the number of her song
& her weave is not a macho thing but circles the warp
O! And then becomes writ in stone

Who shall read them?

going down
saying something confusing
something you meant to say way back it was midnight & you talk it to
    a wall—
old stones, the last blocks hundreds of miles away whisked here on
    whose authority?
I was in love with the heroes & adventurers who quested your dark
    continent

in A Red Notebook
& this was the chaos of the Red Notebook:

storms, conflagration, the tempest at Tulum, hoping to make love in
the water, a nest of hammocks, some hippies still traveling through,
running naked into the water, left a prissy white jacket on the shore,
the kind you wear when the Pope's in town, forgotten in the tequila
of love & dream, silky sand, and the Pope was converting all the sins
to gold pesos under a rim of a saucer go gently here. So what is the
big buck of this town or time?

a little tourism, a little rope hemp but market dries up, one thing re-
places another replaces another, and nylon is the order of the day to
tie anything up replaces another replaces another

This is the red notebook speaking, lifetimes away, sentences freeze in
her handkerchief also the degrees climb. I was planning this notebook
about the new world ways about the rage of any underclass anywhere
you turn, going down to market....

Red because of passion
Red because of blood let
Red in the nature of clay, which card is up
Red because you lied
Red I did your name in red
Red the spotlight was never going to turn
Red was mortified
Red was a palace of seduction & held the breasts aloft
What red could hold artistic attention, hold the crown
Ruby tooth of the jaguar
Priests could sanctify the ball game though it end it must in pain
Eyes turn
It is over
They lose
& Jays & Sox are caught in Oct 1993, Sox lose
You dream or you believe?
Who will win?
Red the color of Philadelphia

Red speaks to a crowd
Red is under seige, a coward
Red in the center of attack
Red in the color glyph code
Coded for centuries
Red whose name is "chac"
EAST WHOSE NAME IS LAKIN
& that is Red's direction: east

Witch, tell my fortune, prophecy my only star
Venus? Do you keep moving or still?

Assignment: dear Naropa students, go again into a museum, stay in
front of a particular picture, graven image, idol or visual detail a long
time. Stay until they close and are restless you leave but don't be rude,
banging the old wooden doors, turning off the fans, you are tired too,
from sleeping on the coast, bugs on the sand, your elegant sun-tanned
legs— —

you stopped in the Museo Arqueológico for rest
down at heels, gorgeous, blond gringa, transfixed in front of the weave
a statue depicting the beginning and end of Maya time
The world directions as discovered by Rosny
& associated colors later by Eduard Seler
& all the deities that crack the whip
Credit where credit is due
Behind the ears? ....in this girl's
    "dig"
& being archeological I unearthed the glyphs to my own rendering
I, Princes am............,she who writes............monkey-scribe...............or
    rabbit woman

    or let me live to crack a code: revolution

went down
went down to the market

What   is   the   best   day   of   the   year
The last day of school, end of school
or 10 years from now, the boy says.........
Life's gonna be different I can go to bars
My mother will be dead
This book will be ancient
I'm not a crystal ball reader, just any psychic out of the street
but son of (child of *yal* (mother)), who borders the next century
----------?----------
He of the wide-mouth speaks it
He is a monkey
2 *yax* he dedicated the *4-bat* place,
    it was his house
        "sky god lord," Moon-skull
            the 7th successor, the lord of the titles, *Yat-Balam*, Holy
                Lord of Yaxchilán (just one example)

Taken?
A problem-solver
Solve the cresent moon
it moves while she   went   down   to.....
her lover, Andros

dark
meteorological dust
settles
on
the
moon's
surface
then
is
covered
by
transparent
oxygen
ice
(I am alone, alone)
Sunlight
penetrates
the ice
&
warms
the
dark material underneath

what market economy lurking there

his *brazos*
arms for the asking only if I feel good, arms for the taking, ordinary
closed eyes, a kiss, detachment of the sense climbing one more pyramid
and wanting to scream How dare you slight the great Jaguar god, how
dare you burn the books in Mani, how dare the colonizer, destroyer of
hemp an old god slighted, down in the teeth, the mouth, the earth

Chac chac chac chac chac chac chac chac chac chac chac chac chac
chac chac chac chac chac ch acch acch acch acch ac

But
the
heat
cannot
escape
through
the
ice
so
some
of
it melts
into
gas
causing
pressure
to
build
until
the
gas
erupts
upwards
through

cracks
chac chac chac chac chac chac chac chac chac chac chac chac chac
  chac chac chac chac chac
carry
I say, carry
ice
&
dark
material
with it
so I go down.............................

she goes down to market
anklets jangle back to----------- India?
   coded back into Ur-language
What are they saying

It is written
It is written

always on my shelf: the terra cotta phallus,
the blood let isn't over yet
I take my cause to Lord Chac

& circle the house of Turtles
the house of the Old Woman
the house of the Dwarves
going down . . .

We went to the Orange Bowl. We took a plane from West Palm to
Miami. It was a two-hour train ride. The train was loaded with Notre
Dame fans. My Dad and I were about the only University of Colorado
fans in our car. When we got to Miami we got on a Subway which
took us to a bus station. From there, a bus took us to a loud Orange
Bowl stadium. We stopped at a stand and bought a cute tee-shirt. My
heart was beating hard. The first thing we saw from our seats was the
Notre Dame Band. They weren't very good, but the Notre Dame fans
liked them. A little kid was screaming his guts out for CU. So was I.
The first half of the game was exciting. The halftime show was pretty
good. It had a lot of firecrackers and lights, dancing and singing and
floats. Then CU kicked off.

The second half was the most exciting part of the game. The game
was over. CU won 10 to 9. CU fans went wild. They were in Heaven.
It was hysterical. It was hard to get out of the stadium. Some were
screaming and some were crying. We tried to find the bus so that we
could get back to the subway station that took us to the train station.
Then we took the train to west Palm Beach.

the men go to the ballgame
she goes down to market

Stephens (my animus in this dream) in Petra, the red city, says to me
you will go you will go there in another calendar & play their games,
unknown then, now ungraspable, you will have to dress like an Arab
boy, & here, the *huipol* (white with flowered embroidery at neck &
hem) or disguise of panama hat, overtime entering
I intrude upon the red ruin and a Menacing Man shows up stealing
    my jewelry
ancient players of the old regime
coming & going
the royals ones absolute in power & pride, they are a writing elite
    named
ah dzib (scribe)

*& then we were driving to Cobá in the little red bug & as I lifted the
    book
to ask had we seen that one, that pyramid yet? you turned for a glimpse
& hit a pot hole, 2 tires blown out*

now at the mercy............

*& the taxi-drivers-who-were-drunk came and asked me to be their amiga
& we pointed to the tires, kaput, and they made motions with their hands
like cars careening out of time & space & huffing noises
so we would get to the repair shop*

*I keep tapping the soberer-one, not at wheel to rein our driver in
almost knocking pedestrians, guys carrying huge goods on bicycles
then
a can-do kid for a few cents fixes the one we had no spare for
his old mother rocking outside, and back to the car safe
we thought we'd end up on the Tzompantli (rack of skulls)*

how out of any of them one reigns supreme?

He was a wise ruler
only sacrificed those he had to

He stopped the clock
He organized the Venus festival
& fixed our tires
with rubber (the blood of trees)
his was the reign of _____
The tablets spoke
you see me, see me calling
& she goes down to the market
no truck in heavenly things
keeps a vision all to herself

Katun 10 Ahau, the Katun is established at Chable.
The ladder is set up over the rulers of the land

the rapport, the bed, the chamber, a cynical conquistador. It was wash
wash wash & wear. I see the colors. I am pink red meat raw & blotched
with a rash of eyes. The scourge of the tourist & her plight, the outline
is political, the outline is insane

It is not dressed up enough in all the colors
Insane?
Because other time-frame. You can get on every wavelength . . .
It is a mere guess how these people, so dark so sophisticated, practiced
    their faith
They say they were obsessed with one eye on their gods
Invoke
Invoke the need for blood
It carries the day
It is mercantile it is slaughter
& went about an ordinary day

They slowed down the process
But the rest of their constituency speeded up
To quit the ground of most resistance
It was ending

I was coming to an end
It was the end of time
It was old hearts cracking
It was a headless body, a woman's....
She had not pitched a ball nor spoke with ill tongue

She had.....................

You have to be in charge, you have to be in charge of *this* body and
putting Anne's brain in this *other* body (someone sent me this dream).
It is a new body for Anne. I may need to repeat: you must put her
brain—it is ashore—in her new body which resembles no one you will
ever know. The poet abdicates control this is a reminder she goes down
to the market..................

so many times to be afraid, your number always comes
you will be flung into the *cenote* one claim to fame
you wanted it
elegant the first time
& entered in
intruder, a clause
a cause for
you wanted it
Did it want you?

Dear Anne,
We were visiting the temple at Ulu Watu. I thought I could fly, out
over the blue green white crashing water. Camera in hand, Grazia was
standing between the outer wall and one of the offering platforms.
Suddenly a monkey jumped from wall to platform using Grazia's shoul-
der as a mid-point springboard. The attendant prevented these quick
grays from proving they're smarter than we are. Dreamt you sobbed
on my shoulder & said, "It's just that I love everyone...."
it's just.......   Love, D.

what generosity rages in death?

On his body, before cremation, little pieces of paper called "armor de-
vis," who are protection devis. No difference between outside & inside
now, why need armor?

It is a long tale, a long drive to the repair shop

Suffice it to say "Paranirvana," holding his seat
  tilt
        rigor mortis a thing of magic
kindness: 49 days
kindness: green mist coming out of mouth
kindness: the tilt of inside & outside
I saw a good king die, a shaman, *h-men,* pass death
in a 20th-century dream
They say blood was pouring from all his pores.......
Though I never needed a sacrificial Patriarch to rule my world

I was never wanton
This was a travel back to gloss & ruins
How the driver-slasher cuts my heart for the scissor cut play
I was dreaming
& then I went down to the market & you said "It's just . . ."
(TV played a role to alternative lore)
Execute half offensive or you be dork, my friend, go around here & I
    am boss
archaic   remote   clues
        shards   p[oint]   o taken!

the slip or shod   harebrained scheme
            vertical flange

ravages   weatherings   layers   obsessed with war

entice   cloud-scroll   austere   how would you
    die?

The Xibalbans hang up twin Hun Hunahpu's head in a calabash tree.
One day a young underworld princess named Lady Blood happens by
& holds her hand up to the head which spits into it. She becomes
pregnant. It's just.......

I screamed
& then died
his arms older than ever, cracked with brown specs (I see it now)
eat eat
drink drink
on this day
dust holds the earth
on that day a blight covers earth
a cloud rises
& mountain too
a strong man seizes the lands
things fall apart
a tender leaf murdered
dying eyes close forever
3 signs on the tree of life
3 generations hang there
the battle cry is raised
They are scattered in the forests

chac chac chac chac

& this is the secret agenda no matter what
(all these in the market place for exchange or sale)
coded: *Itzamna*, Lizard House, one of the aged gods, smokes cigars,
& wears the headdress in the form of a mythological owl-like bird
named *Oxlahun Chan*
His rule of underworld Xibalba is chronicled by the rabbit scribe

rabid scribe

coded: *Ix-chel*, his consort, is moon goddess with a toothless mouth

& finally, Personified Perforator, a stack of 3 knots
Flint, obsidian, thorn, stingray spine are attached to the ubiquitous
    long-nosed head
This deity personifies inanimate objects in the Maya symbol system
& their starry machinations,
that they swept a night sky clean
        close observation, tracking,
                to bring the cosmos to its knees
& rule without & within,
drugged, simply?
living in tandem

a people, whose people, imploded in the Maya tongue

who reads them now
what thought to who stoked the ancestor dream how it was loaded with
    the romance of schemers
& adventurers,

coming down to a power America

& have I told you about the dream, "just a tortilla lady" who visits or
rather I visit her I inhabited some years ago—that skin, that body,
that curious mind, & traveling & she shows me the magical blanket
that weaves itself into the night sky

cordillera, her spine
a shawl to hang about the moon

then rain
it rained
it rained
rain (May-November)
and what was considered in the great span

became
milpas
beans, squashes
sweet manioc, chilli peppers

along the Puuc chain
she went down into the cenote (*dzonot*)
the circular sink hole,
found her death rattle there
found her rapture there
walked the land & talking

spider monkey, howler monkey, ocellated turkey
joined her there
& she wore in her vision
the resplendent pelt of the jaguar
that shone in the moonlight
& her vision was mouthed & recorded by rabbit and monkey twins

it was 23 December AD 2012
when the present universe was annihilated
when the great Cycle of the Long Count reached completion

it is written

They were bled
Who reads them now?

idzat
"artist"

Credo

I want to live the state of "co-emergent wisdom," an old Tantric notion resembling "negative capability." Yet out of that same eye comes research and conviction. I could sing & dance it, the ambiguity of "both, both." The hallmark of our linguistic revolution this century & beyond is that meaning is not simply something "expressed" or reflected in language but is actually PRODUCED by it. I live inside the language of my making, of your making. I'm not interested in the tongue of discursive mind that tides itself against the beautiful increments of experience. I'm interested in the phones & phonemes *of* experience, the language moment to moment, not the concept of my experience. Or yours. Immediate concerns are love—*boddhicitta* (or tenderheartedness) and *prajna* (knowledge—the experiential kind). As female, I am forever adorning empty space. Dressing & undressing. Putting it on & taking it off. Form & emptiness. "Life doesn't seem worth living unless one's on the transforming of energy's side" (Gary Snyder) vibrates for me daily. A **body poetics & politics,** right now. Every syllable is conscious. So enjoy possibility of being alive in the work & as performer of it & with others in community of like-minded-in-body practitioners. We need more instruments of discourse, regular convenings of the tribe. Demons inside need to be expelled as well as terrorists in Washington, or wherever. Global poetics. By all accounts this is only the beginning of the post-modern Dark Ages, *ergo* more light! More poems! More light!

> —*The Jack Kerouac School of Disembodied Poetics*
> *Year of the Water Bird*

photograph by Gary Mackender

About the Author

ANNE WALDMAN grew up on MacDougal Street in New York City, graduated from Bennington College, was an assistant director and director of the Poetry Project at St. Mark's-in-the-Bowery Church from 1966 to 1978, founded (with Allen Ginsberg) the Jack Kerouac School of Disembodied Poetics at the Naropa Institute in Boulder, Colorado, in 1974, has published more than thirty pamphlets and books of poetry, edited Angel Hair Magazine & Books (with Lewis Warsh), Full Court Press (with Ron Padgett & Joan Simon), Rocky Ledge Cottage Editions and Magazine (with Reed Bye), and has edited three anthologies of writing from the Poetry Project, including *Out of This World* (Crown/Random House, 1992). She has also edited *Nice to See You: Homage to Ted Berrigan*, and *Disembodied Poetics: Annals of the Jack Kerouac School*, with Andrew Schelling (University of New Mexico Press, 1994). She has collaborated with a range of artists, including Elizabeth Murray, Red Grooms, Yvonne Jacquette, Joe Brainard, and George Schneeman. A celebrated "performance poet," she works extensively with dancers and musicians. She has performed her work in India, Nicaragua, Berlin, Amsterdam, and Prague, as well as across the United States and Canada. She has made numerous recordings and videotapes, including *Uh-oh Plutonium!, Eyes in All Heads, Live at Naropa*, and *Battle of the Bards*. She has taught at the New College of California, Stevens Institute of Technology, and the Institute of American Indian Arts in Santa Fe. She is on the faculty of the Schule für Dichtung in Vienna. She currently directs the Department of Writing & Poetics at the Naropa Institute, which hosts an annual summer writing program. She is two-time winner of the Heavyweight Championship Poetry Bout in Taos, New Mexico. A practicing Buddhist and "magpie scholar," she has lived and traveled for periods in India and Bali.

PENGUIN POETS

Paul Beatty
Joker, Joker, Deuce

Ted Berrigan
Selected Poems

Jim Carroll
Fear of Dreaming

Amy Gerstler
Nerve Storm

Robert Hunter
Sentinel

Derek Mahon
Selected Poems

Anne Waldman
Kill or Cure

811.54   Waldman, Anne,
WAL   1945-

         Kill or cure.

$14.95

DATE			

11/94   BAKER & TAYLOR